£17.50

2

D0279751

DIRECTORS IN PERSPECTIVE

General editor: C. D. Innes

Peter Stein

What characterizes modern theatre above all is continual stylistic innovation, in which theory and presentation have combined to create a wealth of new forms – naturalism, expressionism, epic theatre, etc. – in a way that has made directors the leading figures rather than dramatists. To a greater extent than is perhaps generally realized, it has been directors who have provided dramatic models for playwrights, though of course there are many different variations in this relationship. In some cases a dramatist's themes challenge a director to create new performance conditions (Stanislavski and Chekhov), or a dramatist turns director to formulate an appropriate style for his work (Brecht); alternatively a director writes plays to correspond with his theory (Artaud), or creates communal scripts out of exploratory work with actors (Chaikin, Grotowski). Some directors are identified with a single theory (Craig), others gave definitive shape to a range of styles (Reinhardt); the work of some has an ideological basis (Stein), while others work more pragmatically (Bergman).

Generally speaking, those directors who have contributed to what is distinctly "modern" in today's theatre stand in much the same relationship to the dramatic texts they work with, as composers do to librettists in opera. However, since theatrical performance is the most ephemeral of the arts and the only easily reproducible element is the text, critical attention has tended to focus on the playwright. This series is designed to redress the balance by providing an overview of selected directors' stage work: those who helped to formulate modern theories of drama. Their key productions have been reconstructed from promptbooks, reviews, scene-designs, photographs, diaries, correspondence and – where these productions are contemporary – documented by first-hand description, interviews with the director, etc. Apart from its intrinsic interest, this record allows a critical perspective, testing ideas against practical problems and achievements. In each case, too, the director's work is set in context by indicating the source of his ideas and their influence, the organization of his acting company and his relationship to the theatrical or political establishment, so as to bring out wider issues: the way theatre both reflects and influences assumptions about the nature of man and his social role.

C. D. Innes

Peter Stein at rehearsal.

Peter Stein

Germany's leading theatre director

MICHAEL PATTERSON

CAMBRIDGE UNIVERSITY PRESS

CAMBRIDGE
LONDON   NEW YORK   NEW ROCHELLE
MELBOURNE   SYDNEY

Published by the Press Syndicate of the University of Cambridge
The Pitt Building, Trumpington Street, Cambridge CB2 1RP
32 East 57th Streeet, New York, NY 10022, USA
296 Beaconsfield Parade, Middle Park, Melbourne 3206, Australia

First published 1981

Printed in the United States of America

Library of Congress catalogue card number: 81-6084

British Library Cataloguing in Publication Data
Patterson, Michael
Peter Stein. – (Directors in perspective)
1. Stein, Peter 2. Theater – Germany (West) –
Production and direction
I. Title   II. Series
792'.0233   PN2658.s/
ISBN 0 521 22442 x hard covers
ISBN 0 521 29502 5 paperback

To Ellinor, Michaela and Yvonne

Contents

Plates

Figures

Tables

Preface

The greatest hope for the German theatre is Peter Stein.   – Fritz Kortner

This volume will examine three aspects of "the greatest hope for the German theatre": the plays that Peter Stein has produced, the structure within which he works and the man himself.

First, Stein has worked on a large variety of plays, from the work of Shakespeare to that of Handke, from German classics to French farce, and to each he has brought originality, intelligence and contemporary perspective. The insights he has discovered in directing these are often more startling and fresh than those derived from traditional modes of drama study which frequently ignore the fact that plays are written for performance. The special advantage that a director like Stein has over the scholar is that he not only proposes a new reading of the text but can also test it in a public situation. It is important to place this research on record.

Secondly, the theatre in which Stein has done most of his work, and which he has contributed most to shaping, is a model of democratic organization. The Schaubühne am Halleschen Ufer (now so famous that it is simply known as the Schaubühne) in West Berlin was reconstituted on participatory lines in 1970. Since then it has explored the advantages and drawbacks of a wholly democratic operation on socialist lines, and has by means of enlightened pragmatism evolved structures that are both efficient and yet give ample scope for critical expression. It is also worth recording this process, since anyone engaged in the debate about the role of political theatre in society or the democratic organization of theatre will find much to reflect on in the experience of the Schaubühne.

Finally, it is important to record the achievements of Peter Stein as a director. Most of the significant innovations in the theatre of this century have come not so much from playwrights as from theatre practitioners. Stanislavsky, Artaud and Brecht (the latter two as directors and theoreticians rather than as writers) have shaped the character of modern theatre more decisively than any dramatist with the possible exception of Beckett. This continues to be the case, but one will have to look far before finding the merest mention in English publications of contemporary German directors like Peter

Stein, Peter Zadek or Claus Peymann, whereas Frisch, Dürrenmatt, Hochhuth, Handke and Weiss have been the subject of numerous books, dissertations and articles. Theatre is the most ephemeral of the arts and, while it is not yet technically possible to preserve a wholly adequate record of the work of a theatre director, this book will try to hold fast something of the genius of Germany's greatest living director, Peter Stein.

MICHAEL PATTERSON

November 1980

Acknowledgments

My thanks go to the following for their help in preparing this volume: Peter Stein himself, Sabine Ganz of the Schaubühne Archives, Rudolf Bergmann of the University of Münster for providing valuable material including an unpublished interview with Stein, Elfriede Irrall, the actress, for her helpful comments on working with Stein, and to Patricia Curran for making available an unpublished interview with Edward Bond.

My acknowledgments for permission to use copyright material go to the following: Bertelsmann Verlag, Munich; BZ, West Berlin; Drama Review, New York; Editions Gallimard, Paris; Eyre Methuen, London; Frankfurter Allgemeine Zeitung; Hanser Verlag, Munich; Kürbiskern, Damnitz Verlag, Munich; Performance, Fort Worth; Die Presse, Vienna; Der Spiegel, Hamburg; Stuttgarter Nachrichten; Suhrkamp Verlag, Frankfurt am Main; Tages-Anzeiger, Zurich; Theater, New Haven; Theater heute, Erhard Friedrich Verlag, West Berlin; Travail théâtral, Lausanne; Die Zeit, Hamburg.

The publisher and I also gratefully acknowledge the permission of the following to reproduce their illustrations in this book: Ilse Buhs for plates 6, 8, 10, 17, 19, and 21; Volker Canaris for plates 2 and 3; Hildegard Steinmetz for plate 1; Ruth Walz for frontispiece and plates 20 and 22–8; Ruth Walz now also handles Helga Kneidl's work and has given permission for plates 4, 5, 12–16, and 18 to be reproduced; Peter Holloway for figures 1–4, 6 and 9–11; the Schaubühne Archives for plate 7 and figures 7 and 8.

It has not been possible to contact Abisag Tüllmann (plates 9 and 11). Her plates have been copied from magazines. If she or her agent will write to the author or publisher, suitable acknowledgment will be made at the earliest opportunity.

1 Exploring styles – Bond's *Saved*, Brecht's *In the Jungle of Cities* and Weiss's *Vietnam-Discourse*

"A new generation in the German theatre," proclaimed the influential West German magazine *Theater heute*, as it awarded its annual accolade of "production of the year" to Peter Stein's staging of Edward Bond's *Saved* in Munich in 1967 (*Theater heute*, 1967/13, p. 57). It was Stein's first professional production and it was "the most astonishing début of any director in the post-war German theatre" (Peter Iden, p. 17).

Stein had had no formal theatre training. Born in Berlin in 1937 the son of a senior industrial scientist, he grew up in the genteel surroundings of the spa-town of Bad Homburg near Frankfurt, where he passed his *Abitur* (school-leaving examination) in 1956. He spent eight years at Munich University (not an excessively long time by German standards), studying literature and fine art "without taking it very seriously." Incapable, by his own admission, of completing a doctorate, he pursued the interest he had already discovered in his work with the student theatre by joining the Munich Kammerspiele in 1964.

His interest in theatre had developed both as spectator and participant. As theatre-goer he had "from 1960 onwards quite deliberately undertaken theatre trips within West Germany, to East Germany and in the whole of Europe" (personal communication, 18 October 1980). As the most important of these experiences he names the Berliner Ensemble production of Brecht's *Arturo Ui*, Besson's productions of Yevgeni Schwarz's *The Dragon* and Molière's *Tartuffe*, Strehler's staging of Brecht's *Galileo* in Milan and "the combined effect of different atmospheric impressions of the theatre in Paris at that time."

His move into the professional theatre was gradual (personal communication, 18 October 1980):

As a student in Munich I acted in short films, trivial pieces for television (children's programmes), I wrote film reviews and above all translated plays from French. From 1959 to 1962 I worked with the Munich student theatre (e.g. I played Heinrich Mann's Bibi and in 1961 directed Musil's *Vincent or the Friend of Important Men*. I then worked with Dieter Giesing as assistant director and *Dramaturg*, and when he joined the Kammerspiele as assistant

1

director, I did free lance work as *Dramaturg* for the Kammerspiele and so eventually managed to get a job there.

The Kammerspiele, one of the major theatres of Munich, had a long tradition of experimentation. It was here that some of the first productions of Strindberg had taken place in Germany (1915 onwards), Brecht, himself a *Dramaturg* at the Kammerspiele, had had his first play performed (*Drums in the Night*, 1922) and had directed himself for the first time (*Edward II*, 1924). In the post-war period the Kammerspiele had again distinguished itself by being the first theatre to perform Dürrenmatt in West Germany and by numbering amongst its directors Fritz Kortner, the grand old man of German theatre. He had been a leading expressionist actor, had performed Brecht in the 1920s and had, as a Jew, been driven into exile by the Nazis.

As a director Kortner was characterized by his rejection of the crude posturing inherited from the Nazi theatre: "The lines were declaimed stiffly, ending with an outburst like a soldier reporting a message. Of course they had gestures: gestures with which they seized the fake sword that hung invisible on their belts" (*Theater heute*, 1970/13, p. 46). In place of these bad habits Kortner insisted on a careful critical reading of the text which was to inform the acting. As the Munich *Dramaturg* Ivan Nagel said of him: "he reads Shakespeare as though it were a sacred text which is to be utterly mistrusted precisely because it is sacred, which can only be appreciated and called into life by combining the deepest respect with the sharpest mistrust" (*Theater heute*, 1967/5, p. 7).

Stein admits that Kortner's influence on him was decisive, and, as we shall see, Kortner's recipe of mistrust and respect characterizes Stein's own theatrical explorations. In particular, Stein learnt from Kortner: precision, clarity, the importance of the word, close observation and untiring concern for detail.

Stein's appointment at the Kammerspiele was as *Dramaturg* and *Regieassistent*, literally "assistant director," but usually in fact in German theatres a very menial post, committing the occupant to perform the trivial tasks that the director cannot be troubled with. It was not until he had already directed *Saved* that Stein was attached to Kortner. "I hear you're a director too," said the older man to him suspiciously at their first meeting. Despite Kortner's geniality, work on his productions proved a hard schooling for Stein: he tells how he was once required to prepare a sound-tape which was to run for a few minutes. It turned out to be a task that took him several weeks, because Kortner repeatedly rejected different recordings. Such fastidiousness and such an uncompromising approach to all aspects of production were lessons that Stein would never forget.

It was in the spring of 1967 that Stein had been given the chance to direct on his own. The play that he chose, Bond's *Saved*, was to have a considerable influence on German playwriting, which until this date had been largely concerned with wider political issues (one thinks of Max Frisch's *Andorra*, Friedrich Dürrenmatt's *The Physicists* or Rolf Hochhuth's *The Representative*). The closest any contemporary German playwright had come to the domestic concerns of ordinary people had been in Martin Sperr's *Jagdszenen aus Niederbayern* (*Hunting Scenes from Lower Bavaria*), 1966, and it was with Sperr that Stein collaborated on a dialect version of *Saved* (*Gerettet*). Traditionally in the German theatre, dialect-plays had been associated with folksy comedies, although occasionally, as with Büchner, Hauptmann and Horváth, dialect had been used with more serious intent. Now, in the politically aware context of the late sixties the attempt was made to provide the proletariat with their own voice.

Of his decision to stage *Saved* Stein says: "With *Saved* I was aware of following in the tradition of the dialect *Volksstück*. I did not really regard this as a particularly new departure, since such plays have always been popular in Munich" (personal communication, 18 October 1980). The production, which opened on 15 April 1967, was the first performance of Bond in West Germany and the beginning of the many successes Bond has enjoyed on German-language stages, to the point that he is now professionally performed there with as much frequency as in Britain.

Martin Sperr's dialect version set out to transfer the original piece from its South London setting to a working-class area of Munich: "How can the theatre seize hold of reality today, if its characters speak a language which they never speak in reality?" queried Sperr (*Theater heute*, 1967/13, p. 74). He was pointing to a problem even more acute in Germany than in English-speaking nations; for German dialects are more akin to distinct languages. At the extreme, a Friesian would fail totally to understand a German-speaking Swiss. The critic Ernst Wendt reported that only 30–50 per cent of Sperr's text was intelligible to him, far less than he would have understood of a performance in French or English. The traditional recourse of playwrights has been to write in the literary language of High German and for actors to render this even more artificial by speaking the text in immaculate *Bühnendeutsch* (Stage German). The gain is supraregional intelligibility; the loss is that the theatre creates a linguistic world of its own, unrelated to the world outside, separated from the lives of the people it is supposedly depicting.

In addition, the style of German actors is often remote from everyday behaviour. Despite the influence of directors like Kortner and the legacy of Brecht's performance style, most German acting would strike Anglo-Saxon audiences as being excessively formal and rhetorical. At its best, it is strongly and uncompromisingly theatrical; at its worst, it is bombastic and empty: a style "which preserves the superficialities, nonsensicalities and hollow emotionalism of expressionist theatre" (Henning Rischbieter, quoted in Daiber, pp. 117–18).

Significantly, Stanislavsky is not at all well known; at the time of writing there are no German editions of his writings in print, and the application of the famous Method is as rare in Germany as it is common in the United States. For this reason the natural and spontaneous style of the young actors in Stein's *Saved* seemed like a new discovery.

The use of dialect also imposed a valuable discipline on the cast: "it made it impossible for the actors to fall back on the acquired emotional and linguistic clichés of Stage German in their portrayal of the characters, and it soon proved to be a hurdle for each false expression and each false gesture" (*Theater heute*, 1967/13, p. 75). From the start, then, Stein was concerned with the primacy of language. Instead of working from preconceived images, he has consistently begun with the word, developing his theatrical treatment from a thoughtful analysis of the author's text.

For some of the cast, like Michael König (Len), who is still today one of Stein's leading actors, it was their first professional role. Pam was played by Jutta Schwarz, who had acted the part at the German-language première in Vienna the previous year, and Martin Sperr himself took the part of Barry. The playing was so natural that the style of the older actors playing Pam's parents seemed "stagey" in comparison.

Stein rehearsed the piece for eight weeks, which is fairly standard for German theatres. Because they had no other commitments, the cast worked in the evenings as well as during the day, so establishing the kind of intensive working schedule for which Stein is renowned. His basic approach was to challenge every expression and gesture to assess whether it was convincing and appropriate, what Stein was later to call "beginning from zero." By this means his cast reached the point where a gap no longer seemed to exist between the actor and the character portrayed. Far from merely acting themselves on stage, however, the actors by hard work and discipline passed through a stage of self-conscious exploration to a higher state of naturalness and so retained an impression of spontaneity while deliberately working to achieve particular effects. So, for example, Jutta Schwarz in Pam's climactic outburst in scene xi was embarrassingly convincing and yet her cries were repeated at the same pitch and rhythm at each performance. As Ivan Nagel commented (*Theater heute*, 1967/13, p. 75):

If Pam's despairing litany ("No 'ome. No friends. Baby dead. Gone. Fred gone.") had merely been an excellently performed theatrical "outburst" instead of the grinding weary and wearying lament of a being who is destroyed and yet insists on being in the right even in her ruin, in which character and actor could hardly be differentiated – then the audience would have been allowed the reassuring possibility of responding with theatre-emotions to the theatre-emotions of the actress.

The same desire to relate the events on stage to reality determined the visual style of the production. Stein and his designer, Jürgen Rose, rejected at an early stage a naturalistic setting, for stage realism in fact weaves an illusion about reality: instead of being confronted by the action on stage, the audience all too easily become mere voyeurs. The common alternative of German theatre, a stylishly abstract set, was also rejected ("the arty-crafty charms of a diluted aesthetic lightness in set-design and set-changes, hessian and bare wood under neon lighting," *ibid.*, p. 76). Instead, Stein and Rose adopted the solution, which derives from Brecht, of making the stage as real (as opposed to realistic) as possible. So, for example, the technical problem of creating the rowing-boat for scene ii was solved by using a real boat, cut off at water level, mounted on concealed rubber wheels and propelled by the actors' feet. A lake in a park cannot be realized on stage; a rowing-boat can.

Thus, while furniture and properties were real, no attempt was made to create the illusion of buildings, trees, and so on. Instead, the wide, shallow stage of the Werkraumtheater (Workshop theatre) of the Kammerspiele (9 m wide by 7½ m deep) was stripped entirely bare. The back of the stage, a 4½ m high wall, was painted in yellow, green, white and silver and was lit by a clearly visible ground row of different coloured lights. In the centre stood a juke-box which blared out pop music during the set-changes. The actors themselves changed the sets on an open stage by bringing on furniture and free-standing flats from the side of the stage where they remained in sight throughout.

1 Bond's *Saved*. Pam (Jutta Schwarz) embraces Fred (Christian Doermer) while Len (Michael König) rows the cut-off boat.

By these means the environment in which the play takes place was created with more conviction than any naturalistic setting would have achieved. The garishly illuminated background and raucous juke-box bombarded the audience with the cheap visual and aural stimuli to which the youths of the play are subjected. Rather than peering in at a way of life, the audience went some way towards actually experiencing it. Indeed, as in London, many of the Munich public rejected this direct confrontation with the violence of their society. The mother of Christian Doermer, the actor playing Fred, herself a well-established actress, walked out during the stoning of the baby, shouting, "I'm not going to put up with my son taking part in this filth."

In Stein's first production, which was an immediate success with the critics if not always with the public, he not only displayed the promise that was to make him one of Germany's leading directors, he also already employed techniques which were to become his standard practice: a long intensive rehearsal period in which he and the cast could explore the text, the questioning of each superficial or hackneyed piece of acting, the insistence on the primacy of the word, the search for reality rather than realism, for clarity in place of mystification. Here, too, in Bond's *Saved*, which ends with an almost wordless scene, Stein first used what has become almost his trademark: an extended piece of silent action on stage. Stein's own summary of his first production could refer to all his work that follows: "Economy was the main requirement in the design and in the acting. Composure and clarity, the invitation to criticize determined the realization of the whole play" (*Theater heute*, 1967/13, p. 75.)

This statement might have come from Brecht, and clearly Stein, both directly and through his mentor Kortner, owes a great deal to

Fig. 1 Bond's *Saved*. The notorious baby-stoning scene, showing the bare stage with juke-box and furniture.

Brecht's influence. The leading Brechtian actress Therese Giehse, whom Stein first met in Munich, regarded Stein as Brecht's true successor (*"Ich hab nichts zum Sagen,"* pp. 154–5 and 196):

Stein is simply the best. Nobody is on a par with him. If Stein knocks over a chair on stage, it is an event; if anyone else does it, then it's just a chair that gets knocked over. . . Stein is a great innovator and emulator: imaginative, honest, painstaking. . . He analyses a play exactly, pulls it apart, dissects it with incredible curiosity. Stein can be really curious. He tries to get to know a play completely. He clarifies the piece, peels off its different layers with all his curiosity and imagination, but he does not change it. The play is there, one has only to bring it alive. Stein does just that. And he is gentle. He slips into his own way of working, so that it is easy to feel at home in his directing style. Rehearsals are easy-going. There's quite a bit of laughter. That's good. You don't have to sweat with effort. Stein has much of the quality of Brecht and has the same way of working . . . As a director Stein is Brecht's immediate successor.

Like Brecht, Stein is an *Aufklärer*, a word related to our own "clear," meaning one who enlightens. Critical clarity is the keynote of the work of both men, not in some cold pseudo-scientific manner but with humour and warmth – a relentless but humble questioning of the world and the theatre that portrays that world.

The major point of divergence between the two directors is determined largely by their historical situation. Brecht spent most of his adult life locked in an ideological struggle against Fascism; Stein's adult life has been spent in the colossal wealth and stability of postwar West Germany. Brecht witnessed capitalism with its kid gloves off and felt bound to take sides vociferously; for Stein the violence of his society remains submerged, and the issues are much more complex. For this reason Stein feels much more at home with the early plays of Brecht than with the didactic tone of the *Lehrstücke.* As he said in an interview with Bernard Dort: "It all seems a bit simple, this mechanistic view of life, the perpetual dialectical motion which Brecht constantly used in his plays – though not so much in his early ones. That is why I prefer them and can hardly imagine what I could do with his later plays" (*Travail théâtral*, 1972, p. 30).

Thus it was that for his next production at the Kammerspiele he chose a little known early play by Brecht, *In the Jungle of Cities.* Begun in 1921 and premièred in Munich in 1923, it had starred Kortner when it transferred to Berlin the following year. It has never been popular, even in the German theatre: Stein's production, which opened on 9 March 1968 as part of the celebrations for Brecht's seventieth anniversary, was only the third professional post-war production of the play.

"The Jungle of Cities" is the gangster world of Chicago in the early years of this century, and the play describes the bitter fight between a Malaysian timber merchant, Shlink, and a downtrodden migrant from the plains, Garga. Why this fight takes place is never explained, and Brecht urges the audience not to look for motives but to "concentrate only on the finish" (preface to the play). The style depends on a deliberate reversal of naturalistic expectations; instead of having past explanations for present behaviour gradually revealed in the manner of Ibsen, the play presents nothing but the process, just as the interest of a boxing-match, from which Brecht's piece takes its idiom, is not in why two men hit each other until one can no longer get up but in the way they conduct their struggle. In terms of ideology, this is perhaps the most nihilistic piece of Brecht's early amoral writing; there is no suggestion in the play that the mutual destructiveness of Shlink and Garga is caused by the contradictions of capitalism. On the contrary Shlink declares to them to be "comrades in a metaphysical undertaking."

On this production Stein worked for the first time with his regular designer, Karl-Ernst Herrmann. Once more the broad stage of the Werkraumtheater was stripped bare, and the action took place amid the hard functional setting of concrete and steel girders. To create different levels and to afford the possibility of simultaneous playing, wooden scaffolding was erected across the width of the stage, and the junk of the city was suggested by oildrums, crates, bottles and litter. On entering the auditorium, the audience were confronted with a film of a boxing-match projected on a screen at the front of the stage. This technique of silent action, typical of Stein's method, was repeated later on stage, when Shlink committed suicide. In Brecht the stage-direction merely says: "He collapses." In Stein's production, Hans Korte as Shlink draped a yellow cloth over himself, lit incense sticks, painted his face white and finally drank poison. Not only was this an extremely theatrical sequence, but it also clarified to some extent the mystery surrounding Shlink's determination to fight Garga to the end: Stein shows Shlink as seeking the ultimate experience of death. As Brecht said at the time of writing the play: "only where death is possible, is there the possibility of pleasure." Appropriately, then, Shlink turned his death into a ritual.

The moment was then suddenly broken by the arrival of a lynch-mob, who pumped Shlink's convulsing body full of bullets, while numerous wooden planks clattered vertically onto the stage from above to form a kind of cage around Shlink's corpse. The final scene with Garga seizing Shlink's money was played as a conclusion of mock-triumph. Garga took the cash-box and climbed to the highest position on the scaffolding, where he received the homage of the rest of the cast. The exaggerated "happy end" threw into question the victory of Garga: in a society based on capitalist competition are there victors or perhaps only victims? It was to be the first of many ironic conclusions that Stein provided for his productions.

Garga was played by Bruno Ganz, who with Edith Clever had come from Bremen to work with Stein. Ganz played Garga with quiet determination and yet with complete physical involvement in the role. The simple directness of his playing, already characteristic of Stein's leading actors, was heightened by the gangster-style attitudinizing of Pavian and Wurm, the latter played by Dieter Laser, who in common with Ganz and Clever was to remain with Stein for several years.

Although *In the Jungle of Cities* had confirmed Stein as one of the most promising new talents in German theatre since the war and the production had been invited to the highly competitive and prestigious Berlin Theatre Festival in June 1968, his career in Munich was to meet an abrupt end. His next production, which opened on 5 July 1968 and which he co-directed with Wolfgang Schwiedrzik, Peter Weiss's *Vietnam-Discourse*, was performed for only three nights; and this was the last time that Stein was to work in the city that had been his home for almost a decade and a half.

Weiss's documentary about the involvement of the United States in Vietnam reveals its content in its full title, *Discourse on the Background and the Course of the Long-lasting War of Liberation in Viet Nam as an Example of the Necessity of Armed Struggle by the Oppressed against Their Oppressors as well as on Attempts of the United States of America to Destroy the Bases of Revolution*. Premièred in Frankfurt in March 1968, it was an intensely topical piece of agitprop theatre, presenting a naive but, given the urgency of the situation, justifiable account of imperialist aggression in Vietnam. Its techniques were those familiar from Piscator and the political revues of the 1920s – caricatured political figures, sometimes presented as puppets with large masks, model situations often performed in mime, and songs with a strong rhythmic beat.

The question that arises from the performance of a political piece like this in a municipal theatre such as the Munich Kammerspiele is: "for whom is this intended?" Since it was presented in the studio and not in the main auditorium and so did not form part of the season-ticket repertory, it was unlikely to attract those who supported US policy in Vietnam. Even if some enthusiast for the struggle of the so-called Free World against Communism had wandered into the Werkraumtheater, it is hardly likely that he would have left the performance shouting in support of Ho Chi-Minh. Unable to reach those who supported US involvement in Vietnam, the piece also said nothing that was not already known, and it is not the primary function of theatre anyway to be the purveyor of information. As one might expect, the young middle-class intellectuals came to the theatre not to be converted nor to be instructed, but to see their views reinforced in an entertaining manner.

Aware of the inefficacy of political theatre, Schwiedrzik and Stein used Weiss's *Vietnam-Discourse* to make this very point. The rear wall of the stage had scrawled across it: "Documentary theatre is crap"; in front of this was a raised platform, on which Weiss's piece was performed, and, stage-left, sat a group of young intellectuals round a café table. They watched the central action, responding predictably and volubly to the points made in Weiss's text. In addition, the well-known satirical singer Wolfgang Neuss acted as a kind of compère, singing songs, making introductions and passing comments on the Vietnam piece and on its left-wing spectators. In addition to a lively presentation of Weiss's piece (especially striking was the scene of politicians planning their strategy like B-film gangsters), the directors went further by challenging the audience rather than massaging their prejudices. Pointing to the group of spectators on stage sitting securely in the material comfort and relative freedom of the West, delighted to be able to display their political awareness by chanting their anti-Vietnam slogans yet powerless to effect any change, Wolfgang Neuss said: "Just look at these people!" and the members of the audience were obliged to look at themselves too.

The events that arose out of this production provided an unfortunate confirmation of the point that Schwiedrzik and Stein were making. The company were committed to the message of the piece (two actors had left during rehearsals because they could not adopt Weiss's position on Vietnam) and so when Neuss proposed that the performance should end with a collection for the Vietcong, this met with unanimous approval. The Director of the Kammerspiele, August Everding, however, banned the collection in the main building, suggesting as a compromise that it might take place on the street outside or at the door of the Werkraumtheater as a private initiative. Neuss insisted on his right to make the collection, and his contract was not renewed. It is difficult to assess the extent of Stein's commitment to left-wing activism at this period, but having just co-directed a piece condemning the merely rhetorical posturing of left-wing intellectuals, he could hardly do other than take sides, and he and Schwiedrzik resigned as an act of solidarity. As they wrote at the end of their "Declaration" (*Theater heute*, 1968/8, p. 32): "The responsibility for cancelling further performances must be that of a schizophrenic theatre management which puts an agitational political piece in the repertory but prevents a performance that draws agitational and political consequences."

For the subsidized theatres of West Germany this was a model case of their willingness to follow the trend of presenting political pieces while insisting that the theatre had no immediate political function. As Schwiedrzik and Stein had sensed, actors and audiences were welcome to condemn aggression in Vietnam, so long as they did nothing about it on theatre premises.

It was the Schaubühne am Halleschen Ufer, later to become Stein's permanent home, that invited the *Vietnam-Discourse* production to Berlin. It seemed an appropriate and generous gesture that a socialist-oriented theatre of the Prussian capital should offer a helping hand to theatre workers who had been thrown out of their place of work in the main city of Bavaria. In the event, however, the Schaubühne experience was merely to furnish further proof of the need for a radical restructuring of the theatre in order to make truly progressive work possible.

The *Vietnam-Discourse* opened on 11 January 1969. "The first night was wild," recalls Stein. The performance which had lasted one and a half hours in Munich now ran for three and a half because of constant interruptions from the audience. These were the heady days of student riots, left-wing street demonstrations and their violent suppression. Theatre-going for the predominantly student audience at the *Vietnam-Discourse* was not a matter of passive entertainment but the opportunity for political analysis and discussion. So now the actors found themselves not only being interrupted with comments about the play but also being challenged to defend their situation as actors, that is, as purveyors of art to the consumer.

Despite the excitement surrounding this and the two subsequent performances, however, it was away from the stage that the real action took place. It began before the opening night when two technicians, whose contracts had already expired and who had been disappointed in their request to work on the *Vietnam-Discourse*, painted anti-American slogans on the walls of the theatre. The two protagonists in this drama were asked to clean their graffiti off the walls and, when they refused, were banned from the theatre. The *Vietnam-Discourse* ensemble declared their solidarity with the technicians and refused to continue rehearsals. Peter Weiss, the author, offered to lend his support by withdrawing the rights of his piece, but these were in fact held by the publishers. After some negotiation the ensemble agreed to continue work on the play. It was also agreed that – in contrast with Munich – the cast would be allowed to collect for the Vietcong. The ensemble, however, decided on an even more provocative course of action by concluding their performance with a collection for American soldiers prepared to desert.

What in Britain might have been regarded patronizingly as an ultimately laughable attempt to affect the course of the war in South East Asia was seen in West Berlin as a real threat from within. It was unthinkable that the Berlin Senate would tolerate for long public money going to a theatre which harboured a group intent on undermining the morale of the US army, for better or worse the major military protectors of the status of West Berlin.

On 16 January, therefore, the Schaubühne Directors decided to remove the *Vietnam-Discourse* from the programme. The ensemble and a number of sympathizers reacted by staging a sit-in at the theatre. The Directors responded by calling in the police. "They behaved absolutely idiotically," recalls Stein, "they simply didn't want to have these unruly children in the building any longer" (unpublished Bergmann interview, 1978). The Berlin police, not noted for their gentleness, rounded up the protesters and held them for five hours at police headquarters before releasing them. In retrospect, the Directors Schitthelm and Weiffenbach view their understandable but nervous over-reaction "self-critically," and ultimately it did not sour relations between them and Stein. Within eighteen months reconciliation was to be total. As Stein says, "That's the way I operate" (*ibid.*).

The incident was therefore of importance not so much in the way it affected Stein's career but for the insights it afforded him into the function and limitations of political theatre. As Bruno Ganz remarked (*Spielplatz* 1 (1972), 53): "Of course, Stein only really woke up as a result of the student riots." In time, however, Stein recognized how self-indulgent the political posturing of the *Vietnam-Discourse* ensemble had been (Schaubühne Protocol no. 494, 8 October 1975): "Looking back on it from this point in time the whole undertaking was inexcusable."

Once the pseudo-revolutionary excitement had abated, Stein was eventually to subscribe to a statement made during the episode by the Directors of the Schaubühne: "In the present social situation theatre can fulfil merely the function of enlightenment but not of revolution."

In his first two years of directing Stein had already explored the major stylistic areas which were to characterize the full range of his work. The last example, the cartoon agitprop style of the *Vietnam-Discourse*, was the least important, too crude a medium for Stein to return to. In *Saved* he had employed a naturalistic acting style which was later to reach its most accomplished form in his production of Gorky's *Summerfolk*. By contrast, in Brecht's *In the Jungle of Cities* he used a much more economical style that was to characterize most of his classical productions, a style that he has described as *"plakativ,"* that is, having the clarity and size of a poster. It is a more theatrical style than naturalistic acting but does not imply a return to the rhetorical tradition of German acting, for it shares with this only its boldness of gesture. It goes beyond it in its intelligence and critical awareness, so that the actor's basic concern is to portray reality while avoiding the distraction of naturalistic trivia.

While it may be convenient to refer to these two divergent styles as naturalistic and Brechtian, Stein has used them in his own very individual manner. *Saved* was non-naturalistic in its setting, and, as we shall see, the focus in *Summerfolk* was as much on the social function of the characters as on any Stanislavskian psychological realism. Similarly, although the boldly economical *plakativ* style owes much to Brecht, Stein distrusts the notion of "alienation" in acting, the insistence that the audience should be constantly reminded that the actor is demonstrating rather than embodying a role. Stein criticized the acting style of the Berliner Ensemble (*Travail Théâtral*, 1972, p. 30):

For me it was too clever, the actors showed too much of what they knew, it was too quick, not intense enough to develop the gest and often too external to express the text, etc. I can't stand the principle of alienation used in this way – it's tripe. When an actor gets up on stage and begins to speak, that is already totally alienating. That's what has to be avoided. Otherwise the audience experiences nothing.

Instead of seeking the demonstrational quality of Brechtian acting theory, Stein encourages his actors to enter fully into the spirit of their roles (as indeed the best Brechtian actors like Busch and Weigel did) without, however, exhausting the possibilities of their performance by merely presenting "characters."

It was this flexibly Brechtian approach that informed Stein's exploration of the classics – not only Schiller, Goethe and Kleist, but also Ibsen and Shakespeare – and it is above all this adventurous treatment of great works of the past on which Stein's reputation is based.

2 The Brechtian approach to the classics – Schiller's *Intrigue and Love* and Goethe's *Torquato Tasso*

In the post-war period in Germany there have been basically three approaches to the performance of classics: first, there is the "archaeological" treatment, the presentation of a great work of the past in a sober, uninventive style, as though it were an exhibit in a museum; secondly, there is the attempt to update the material, usually by adopting modern dress and manners, inspired by a Romantic belief in the "eternal quality of the work of art"; thirdly, there is the method, derived from a proper understanding of Brecht, of "appropriation," in which the preoccupations of a work of the past are not wrenched from their social and political context but are examined in that context to discover what points of relevance can be found for our own time.

It was this method of appropriation that was to distinguish Stein's treatment of the classics. As Bruno Ganz, who played the title-role in *Tasso*, said of the play (*Torquato Tasso. Regiebuch der Bremer Inszenierung*, p. 138):

The awareness of living two hundred years later has never made itself so strongly felt in working on a classic as with *Tasso*. I should like to try to make a basic point about this remoteness. Usual production method: the remoteness gets in the way, work suffers. Such producers take it for granted that they have to "get over" this problem (e.g. modernization). The more meaningful and honest approach however would be to create a dialectical relationship between the remoteness and the material. We should not suppress the remoteness but become aware of it as the starting-point.

Already, as guest director in Bremen, Stein had drawn on the tension between historical context and modern relevance in his staging of Schiller's *Kabale und Liebe* (*Intrigue and Love*), which opened on 7 November 1967. Stein had seen Kortner's production of the play at the Kammerspiele in 1965 and regarded his own version as a "productive response" to it, not as an attempt to improve on Kortner: "Since I have been going to the theatre, I have never had the feeling, 'I could do that better myself' " (Personal communication, 18 October 1980).

Intrigue and Love was Schiller's third play, written in 1784 when he

15

was still in his revolutionary "Storm and Stress" period before turning to the wider historical issues of his mature writing. Briefly, it deals with a love-triangle: Luise Miller, a bourgeoise girl, is loved by a young nobleman, Ferdinand, who in turn is loved by an aristocratic courtesan of great sensibility, Lady Milford. The element of intrigue is introduced by the machinations of Ferdinand's father and his secretary, Wurm, to prevent Ferdinand from marrying beneath his class. The play ends tragically with Ferdinand killing Luise and himself by putting poison in a glass of lemonade.

The play veers close to the melodramatic. It contains high-flown language, characteristic of the emotional tenor of the "Storm and Stress", and Ferdinand in particular is highly strung and impetuous.

Stein found the point of relevance in Schiller's play by concentrating on the "love" of the title rather than on the "intrigue." Clearly, the social dimensions of the play, the virtual impossibility of Ferdinand marrying a commoner, the whole background of the court with its cynical manoeuvrings, none of these seems of much moment to a modern audience. Admittedly, class structure persists today and politicians are still not renowned for their integrity, but the specific political and social concerns are undeniably those of Schiller's period. So it was not at this point that Stein attempted to engage the interest and sympathy of his audience. Instead he demonstrated the perennial theme of the vulnerability and destructiveness of love, of love that makes uncompromising demands on the world, of love that must succumb because the real world will not accommodate these demands. If there was a contemporary political message in the play, it was addressed to the youthful idealists of Germany, whose impatient demands that the world should change erupted in the student revolts of 1968 and met with opposition from right-wing authority and left-wing establishment alike.

Paradoxically, then, to make his piece more relevant, Stein played down the more overtly political elements in it. Ferdinand's father, the President, seemed motivated by boredom rather than expediency. His secretary, Wurm, traditionally played as a Machiavellian schemer, was presented by Bruno Ganz as a precise and willing bureaucrat, his hair smooth and neat, the sleeves of his coat too short for him. The concentration instead was on the three "lovers." Lady Milford was played as an astonishingly young and sensitive woman, who had had her fill of being the Duke's mistress and was now consumed by a deep and genuine passion for Ferdinand. When she begged Luise to renounce her love for Ferdinand, she threw herself full-length at Luise's feet – an uncompromising expression of her total love, typical of the physical involvement of Stein's performers.

Michael König, as Ferdinand, was directed by Stein to avoid the obvious danger of making the character an eighteenth-century "angry young man." Several of Schiller's more magniloquent lines were cut, and König played the part with simple directness. Instead of ranting, he, like most of the cast, spoke slowly and quietly, sometimes barely audibly, so that the words seemed like a desperate search for expression, as though language might at any moment fail to give shape to feelings.

The most outstanding performance was given by Edith Clever as Luise. As Georg Hensel enthused: "Whoever has seen the Bremen production of *Kabale und Liebe* will have seen, heard and understood why Schiller originally called his play *Luise Millerin*. This unpretentious mouse-like girl dominates the stage. I have never seen such crouching, such writhing, such a turning into itself of a wounded creature" (*Theater heute*, 1968/13, p. 130).

Jürgen Rose's set matched the economy and intensity of the acting. The Millers' living-room had a minimum of furniture and props, no naturalistic clutter to suggest the bourgeois household, but rather a drab neatness. Wurm's office was created simply with table and chairs, and even the more luxurious setting of Lady Milford's chamber was austere: a large window ran across the back of the stage, there were a few pieces of elegant period furniture, and only the fine pastel blue curtains that spilled overlong onto the floor suggested any kind of aristocratic extravagance.

Returning to Bremen after the double failure of the *Vietnam-Discourse*, Stein had reason enough to examine the function of theatre in West Germany of the late 1960s, and it was in Bremen that this self-questioning about the meaning and effectiveness of theatre found its theatrical expression. On 30 March 1969 Stein's strikingly new interpretation of Goethe's *Torquato Tasso* opened at the Theater am Goetheplatz, Bremen. It was Stein's most ambitious project until then and the first time that he had tackled a major classic. It was also the production that was to cause the greatest controversy over Stein's work, with views ranging from those hailing it as "the most thoughtful and exciting production in Germany for years" (Botho Strauss, *Tasso-Regiebuch*, p. 167) to those that dismissed it as "neither good nor meaningful, not enlightening and certainly not true" (Joachim Kaiser, *Theater heute*, 1969/13, p. 23).

Goethe is the literary giant of the German nation, and *Torquato*

2 Goethe's *Tasso*. Tasso (Bruno Ganz) as "emotional clown" presents his art for the approval of his aristocratic patrons, Leonore (Edith Clever), Princess (Jutta Lampe) and Duke (Wolfgang Schwarz).

Tasso, after his *Faust* and *Iphigenie auf Tauris,* is his third most important work for the stage. Completed in 1789, it is cast in the classical mould, observes the unities, and is written in mellifluous blank verse. The central figure, Torquato Tasso, is court poet to Duke Alfons II of Ferrara. When he gives his epic poem on the liberation of Jerusalem to the Duke, the Princess, sister to the Duke, crowns him with a laurel wreath. To her acclaim is added the praise of the Countess Leonore Sanvitale. Tasso's happiness, however, is threatened by the arrival of Antonio, the Duke's Secretary of State, an efficient but cold diplomat. Rivalry develops between Tasso and Antonio until the point where Tasso, in fury at Antonio's taunting words, draws a sword on him. The Duke intervenes and orders Tasso to confine himself to his room. Tasso feels betrayed by the court, above all by the Princess whom he loves. Through the intercession of Leonore and Antonio, Tasso is reconciled with the Duke but begs leave to depart from Ferrara for a while. On parting from the Princess, however, Tasso loses his self-control once more and embraces her passionately. The Duke and the two ladies finally repudiate him, and Tasso turns in desperation to Antonio – like a shipwrecked sailor clinging to a rock.

Tasso is in many ways a personal account by Goethe of his own life at the court of Weimar. As he said, it was "bone of my bone and flesh of my flesh." Seen in this autobiographical light, the main concern of the play is with the attempt by Goethe to reconcile the poetic and undisciplined side of his nature with the practical demands of courtly life, to unite the spiritual man with the man of activity. It is in this way that the play has been traditionally presented on stage: Tasso as a suffering artist figure, a man at odds with the world around him. It is his environment that is regarded as the norm, the system of patronage is taken for granted and, despite his genius, it is Tasso who must learn to conform or "drown."

With the scepticism learned from Kortner and enlightened by his own experiences of West German theatres, Stein evaluated Goethe's text in an original way. In his view patronage was anything but an acceptable system: in the feudal court of Goethe's Ferrara artistic creations were reduced to luxury consumer goods, and Tasso was given the role of "emotional clown." Stein considered that the artist shared this same basic sense of alienation in contemporary bourgeois society. Like Tasso, the actor receives applause from his audience but is distrusted as soon as he attempts to involve himself in real life, in the world of politics. Like Tasso, Stein was acclaimed for his early productions but was banished as soon as he participated in active gestures to support what he had propagated on stage. As with Tasso, too, these gestures had in their impotent anger a comic, almost farcical quality.

In order to tear through the veil of classical perfection, to reveal clearly the "real," that is, social circumstances of the play, Stein with his *Dramaturg*, Yaak Karsunke, embarked upon the first of the major textual adaptations for which Stein has become renowned. Although very modest about his versions of established texts ("I do my so-called adaptations sitting on the toilet"), Stein reveals in them careful thought and a sensitive ear. Generally speaking, the process is one of cutting and editing. Seldom is a word uttered on stage that does not belong to the original, but speeches or whole scenes may be re-arranged, lines given to another character and endings in particular modified.

In the case of *Tasso*, the original was felt to be too long and the writing often too decorative, so about a quarter of the lines were cut: "in our version we cut primarily poetic lines. The role of the [poet's] employer was retained" (*Tasso-Regiebuch*, p. 136). The editing consisted of breaking down the five acts of Goethe's play into ten episodes, with a prologue and two "interludes." The episodes, each with its title (e.g. "The Quarrel," "Antonio's Opinion," "Faux-Pas"), follow the order of events in Goethe's plot and, with few exceptions, the lines are spoken in their original sequence. It is in the prologue and interludes that the editing is most daring. The prologue introduces the five characters of the play by means of typical statements drawn from the first and second acts of the original. This collage technique replaces the measured flow of expositional dialogue with juxtaposed declarations, for example, Tasso on his poetry, Leonore on Ferrara, the Princess on her youth. This, together with the montage effect of the interludes, where passages of dialogue are again presented as monologues, clearly owes a great deal to Brecht's epic theatre, as do the episodes with their "Brechtian" titles.

In what Brecht describes as "dramatic" or "Aristotelian" theatre the action develops in a linear fashion, by means of which the audience becomes convinced of the inevitability of the progression of events. In his own proposal for an "epic" theatre Brecht wished that the action should invite critical assessment, that it should proceed by leaps rather than by deterministic causality; so he structured his pieces as a montage of episodes rather than as a sequence of inter-locking scenes. By applying an epic treatment to the plot of *Tasso*, Stein in the very structure of his version threw the smooth and consequential development of Goethe's work into question. No longer was the audience to accept the manner in which Tasso is treated in Ferrara, but by weighing statement against statement and episode against episode it was invited to evaluate critically the established norms of the social context. By undermining the absoluteness of the play's dramatic structure, Stein challenged the absoluteness of the social structure it reflected.

In addition to the critical analysis provided by this textual arrangement, the editing of the prologue in particular accords well with the techniques of modern dramaturgy: it becomes justified on aesthetic as well as ideological grounds. In the wake of Brecht and Artaud, contemporary playwriting has generally abandoned the leisurely exposition of Goethe's age in favour of a series of images, reminiscent of the montage and cross-cutting of the cinema.

The setting of the play reinforced Stein's critical approach to the text. In order to signal to the audience that Goethe's concern with Tasso related to his own situation at Weimar and might therefore also have application to contemporary society, Stein set the play not in Renaissance Italy but in Goethe's Germany. The busts of Virgil and Ariosto of the original were replaced by a single bust of Goethe himself, and the costumes were approximately of the Biedermeyer period, although Tasso's knee-breeches had a more archaic quality than the straight trousers of the Duke and Antonio, and the flowing gown of the Princess and heavy brocade of Leonore looked forward to the luxuriant images of Gustav Klimt.

The Bremen designer, Wilfried Minks, suggested the opulence of the court of Ferrara by covering the large stage with a deep-pile carpet in various shades of green. By using the natural colours of grass in the luxurious artificiality of a carpet, the set reflected the tension between nature and civilization which is one of the major themes of the play: like the artificial constraints Tasso is supposed to impose on his natural impulses, the carpet represents nature tamed – a lawn that is ever devoid of mud. To the rear and sides of this large open area were erected perspex screens through which shimmered dull gold walls and pillars. Because entrances were concealed, the screens gave the impression of completely enclosing the acting area, so that the actors seemed to be trapped within their setting – in the best tradition of the classical theatre. At the same time the transparency of the perspex suggested the vulnerability of this enclosed society.

There was hardly any furniture: a chair for the Duke, and a table and a chair for Tasso. As in his Munich productions, Stein favoured a broad open stage with a minimum of dressing. Moreover, in the tradition of Brecht, full white lighting was maintained throughout.

In typical Stein manner the play opened with a silent sequence. Bruno Ganz as Tasso was seen adopting self-congratulatory poetic poses, at one point directly imitating the famous Tischbein portrait of Goethe. Gathering his cloak about him he went to sit on his chair, but – since he was staring into the distance in deep poetic contemplation – missed the chair and ended sitting on the floor. This moment symbolized Stein's "dethronement" of Goethe as an object of false respect. The comedy was by no means gratuitous but a means of distancing the audience from the self-indulgent suffering of Tasso: it was not so much a product of his "artistic soul" as of his social situation. This clumsiness and exaggeration were repeated at other points in the play: when Tasso received his laurel wreath from the Princess it seemed to weigh him down; he peered up cross-eyed at this burden on his brow. To avoid Tasso's embrace, Antonio stepped back suddenly causing Tasso to sprawl at his feet. As Tasso slashed

Fig. 2   Goethe's *Tasso*. Wilfried Minks's set, showing Tasso at his table, the Duke slumped in his chair, the Princess sitting left foreground, and Leonore kneeling beside Antonio. The bust of Goethe stands behind them.

wildly at Antonio with his sword, the Duke walked calmly between them, making Tasso's attack seem utterly harmless and pathetic. The final act of ineptitude was what Stein entitled "faux-pas": Tasso, declaring his love for the Princess, attempted to embrace her. As he clasped her round the waist, she leant back, her head almost disappearing into the high folds of her cloak. In desperation Tasso tried to climb up on her, first with one leg, then with the other. When he let go, she fell backwards and Tasso fell backwards the other way – a piece of slapstick, whose humour was undermined by the shocked intervention of the Duke and Tasso's pathetic withdrawal clutching the discarded cloak of the Princess. As Bruno Ganz summarized his intentions in this episode: "Tasso is allowed to pay courtly love to the Princess, but touching her leads to catastrophe" (*Tasso-Regiebuch*, p. 147).

The final image of the play also grotesquely combined humour with pathos. After Tasso's famous concluding speech comparing himself to a shipwrecked mariner clinging to the rock of Antonio, Ganz clambered up onto Werner Rehm's shoulder. He squatted there, looking back over Rehm's head with the mindless complacency of "a monkey who has just neatly completed its turn and is being carried off by its trainer" (Botho Strauss, *Tasso-Regiebuch*, p. 163).

By treading the dangerous path of inviting the audience to laugh at Tasso, Stein demystified the original, making the issues clearer than in any other contemporary staging of the piece. Botho Strauss spoke of Stein's "exaggeration for the sake of clarity (in the manner learned from Kortner) of obviously insufferable, paradoxical or idiotic conditions" (*ibid.*, pp. 162–3). This clarity extended to the way each individual line was spoken. It was evident that each actor shared an awareness of the intentions of the production (this was shown by their responsiveness as a group to questions asked about it), and this awareness informed the delivery of the lines. Once again Stein worked with precision on the text, generating images from the spoken word rather than from a private vision of the play. Ivan Nagel described Stein's method (*Tasso-Regiebuch*, pp. 184–5):

Having revealed language in its most general function as the self-protective cocoon of the ruling class, having determined from this the specific dramatic value it has for each of the five characters, he undertakes a line by line examination of the actual content of this sententious blank verse . . . He takes Goethe at his word who maintains that all his characters preserve the elevated form in every one of their sentences – that for them the uncommon is commonplace. This idealistic conversation (the magically protected homogeneity of elevated speech and response) must now be put to the test, must be confronted with the intonation which its actual content would demand in everyday conversation.

So, for example, Edith Clever as Leonore created a critical distance from the elevated tone of Goethe's verse by speaking the lines in a manner entirely appropriate to the content but at such odds with the form that it "had a grotesque and blasphemous shock-effect" (ibid., p. 185). Speaking of her son, she clucked with as much maternal pride as any of the German matrons in the Bremen audience would have shown; speaking to Tasso of the Princess, her tone became that of a jealous woman scheming to make a younger rival seem less attractive; her advice to Tasso to leave Ferrara was spoken with such maternal gentleness that it sounded like a self-evident truth.

Similarly, the sing-song quality of Jutta Lampe's delivery of the Princess's lines pointed to the delicate decadence of her character and again invited the audience to listen with scepticism to her utterances. As Lampe said of the relationship of the Princess to her "suffering": "She loves and enjoys it, she nurtures it. This cultivation of suffering, this willingness to take upon herself what is called Fate, is a constant excuse for doing nothing" (Tasso-Regiebuch, p. 148). In the second act Tasso expounds to her his vision of the Golden Age, ending with his dream of innocent permissiveness: "Erlaubt ist, was gefällt." ("Whatever gives pleasure is good.") The Princess counters this by relegating the Golden Age to a distant past and proposes a different moral criterion: "Erlaubt ist, was sich ziemt." ("Everything that is seemly is good.") Traditionally this line has been delivered as though through it Goethe was championing classical propriety as the means of restoring the Golden Age, as a necessary corrective to Tasso's hedonism. But Goethe is weighing issues and not delivering messages; Lampe's treatment of the line, as an almost coquettish declaration of her conformity to a society that stifles natural impulses, restored the balance in the debate between her and Tasso. As Nagel observed, her statement is "the formula of her capitulation, which she now wishes to impose on the one person who might threaten her capitulation" (Tasso-Regiebuch, p. 182).

The natural delivery of the lines was less easy for the Duke (Wolfgang Schwarz) and Antonio (Werner Rehm), since their task was to embody the rigid formality of the court. But nevertheless even here one was aware that lines were part of a dramatic dialogue, that they reflected character and attitude, and were not being rendered conventionally as autonomous poetry.

3   Goethe's *Tasso*. Tasso (Bruno Ganz) "as a monkey . . . carried off by
its trainer," Antonio (Werner Rehm).

The four figures round Tasso also in a sense provided him with an audience. For much of the play all five actors were on stage at the same time (even Antonio spoke in the prologue although his arrival in Ferrara occurred later in the play). Frequently they listened to Tasso's monologues, and on one occasion applauded a particularly vehement outburst with a silent hand-clap. The manner in which society emasculates the artist was shown by his vulnerability – Tasso's table set in the open space round which his aristocratic patrons idly drifted – and by the ease with which they reduced his passionate effusions to yet another artistic product to be enjoyed.

Thus Bruno Ganz did not identify with Tasso but "quoted" him, and one is reminded of the fifth of Brecht's "Instructions to the actor": "Instead of trying to create the impression that he is improvising, the actor ought rather to show the truth – that he is quoting." Indeed the replacement of a psychological approach to acting by an analysis of the social dimensions of a role owes much to Brecht's example. Bruno Ganz, for example, found points of identification with Tasso not through uncritical empathy but in a parallelism of their situations (*Tasso-Regiebuch*, p. 139):

In the scene where I was crowned with a laurel wreath I felt "personally involved" when I recalled how I react to the praise of the public, of theatre management and directors. In this way I could empathize with Tasso by recognizing that there is only a formal difference between Tasso's dependence on Duke Alfons and my own dependence on the theatre management.

Edith Clever in an interview gave an extensive answer to the question whether her critical awareness had been strengthened during her work on *Tasso*. It provides excellent insights into the direction that Stein and his actors were moving in terms of both their work on stage and the structure of their working conditions (*Tasso-Regiebuch*, pp. 150–1):

An actor is trained for a purely psychological not a critical approach. It begins at drama school. In each role he sees its tragic quality; the weaker the character, the more attractive it is; the actor plunges into the abyss. He does not attempt to demonstrate the possibility of change in people and conditions, he merely attempts to arouse a sentimental understanding. An actor has to be grateful for each engagement, for each role. He is reduced to displaying feelings and representing "humanity," he is never forced or encouraged to think independently, so that he is allowed more or less to act the fool. He is permitted moods but not serious demands.

Most actors, apart from the privileged few, who are better at hiding the fact, are engaged in a constant struggle to survive. They have to be successful with the public, the director, the theatre management, their own colleagues etc. If they do not wish to accept a role, they will at best be compelled by the argument that they should have the interests of the theatre at heart. They are not invited to discussions about the programme. And even costumes are forced on them, if the director insists. So every actor dreams of becoming a star himself in order to have more rights. That is to say, he is seeking power.

Through working on *Tasso* I recognized that these conditions can be altered, that they must not necessarily be like this.

In the words of this highly articulate actress one can already recognize the search for a new theatre form which was to lead directly to the establishment of the reformed Schaubühne am Halleschen Ufer. In this sense *Tasso* was not only a remarkable production of a classic but also a considerable contribution to the current debate on theatre reform.

Uncertain whether the critical presentation of *Torquato Tasso* would in itself suffice to make the intended points about the alienation of the artist, Stein and his ensemble turned to a more immediate method of communication by reading prepared statements in the interval. Significantly, each actor and even the usually downtrodden *Regieassistent* wrote his or her own statement and read it out, while the director remained silent. The content of the statements concerned Tasso's role as paid "clown" of his feudal court and attempted to relate it to the concerns of contemporary society. Bruno Ganz asserted (*Tasso-Regiebuch*, pp.124–5):

The lack of freedom which we experience as artists is not basically different from the lack of freedom you experience in your work. Like you . . . we have to deliver the goods and like most of you we cannot determine the use or effect of our work . . . We consider that the conflict portrayed in *Tasso* is not exclusively confined to the artist or the genius but is a problem shared by everybody who works in a system where one is ruled from above.

One wonders how a Bremerhaven dock-worker, had he mistakenly entered the theatre that night, might have responded to Ganz's association of his problems with those of a labourer; undoubtedly the rebuff would have been considerably more vehement than that from the "ruling class." Even the office-workers in the audience might have wondered at this invitation to seek points of identification with the specific problems of a rather neurotic young poet.

Admittedly, the ensemble had reason enough to be aware of the limitations on its working freedom. The night before the première of *Tasso* an extraordinary piece of "theatre" had taken place. For two months previously a collective of actors, with the approval of Kurt Hübner, the *Intendant* or Director of the Bremer Theater, had been working on a production of Aristophanes' *Parliament of Women*. Without director or other authority they had been attempting to stage the piece as an exercise in co-operative democracy. However, the collective, amongst whom were numbered Michael König and Sabine Andreas, understandably became more involved in questions regarding the process than in the finished product. When the audience arrived for the première, they were astonished to discover that in place of the advertised play the actors had simply arranged benches on the stage and invited the public to debate questions of the theatre with them. During the discussion, Hübner clambered around on the catwalks in the lighting rig, shouting down comments and objections from his vantage-point in the darkness above the participants' heads, unintentionally providing a potent symbol of the remote authority of the traditional *Intendant*. Not altogether unreasonably Hübner cancelled further "performances" of *The Parliament of Women,* and once more Stein and his ensemble resigned in solidarity. This was to be Stein's last production in Bremen, the end of a potentially fruitful collaboration with Hübner and a further impetus to find a theatre where the experiment of collective production would not only be tolerated but encouraged.

Stein's ensemble therefore once more felt themselves oppressed and no doubt honestly believed that their situation corresponded with that of, say, a worker on the factory floor. In fact, their production of *Tasso* in its very brilliance, its almost hermetic perfection, became virtually as autonomous a piece of "fine art" as Goethe's original.

Moreover, the risks so boldly taken in a critical view of the play could easily tip over into parody. The difference between criticism and parody is that in the former actor and audience challenge the conventional respect afforded to the original in order to penetrate to a more substantial truth; in the latter the conventional respect is demolished in order to provide supercilious amusement. In the one the spectator says, "I will see beyond this"; in the other he says, "I have grown beyond this." Significantly, after its initial success in Bremen, the production was invited to the "experimenta" Theatre Festival in Frankfurt in June 1969. The festival audience, ever eager for cleverness and novelty (this was the scene of Handke's first triumphs), found this "new-look" Goethe hilarious, and the performance slipped into the superficial parody over which it had been walking its tight-rope. Snarling reviews followed, Stein was denounced as a "protest-clown," but none of this prevented *Tasso* from becoming the most frequently performed of all Stein's early productions: sixteen performances in Bremen, fifteen in Zurich, seven guest performances, including Venice and the Berlin Theatre Festival, and finally thirty-four performances to open the new Schaubühne am Halleschen Ufer – a total of seventy-two performances, which, while hardly comparing with the long runs of Broadway or the West End, is impressive by German standards.

The major achievement of Stein's *Tasso*, if one discounts the somewhat narcissistic concern of the theatre with its own function, was Stein's ability to employ a tough Brechtian critical approach without resorting to Brecht's "rough theatre." With an astonishingly sure hand Stein combined political analysis with an exquisitely polished aesthetic product. Small wonder that he was distrusted not only by the establishment on which he had declared war but also by socialist elements who were to regard Stein's striving for artistic quality as in some way a betrayal of revolutionary attitudes.

For Stein, *Tasso* showed the possibilities of collective work with a dedicated and intelligent ensemble. It also showed that his conventional approach as autocratic director needed to be subjected to revision. Seven years later he was to say (*Theater heute*, 1976/13, p. 12):

I no longer work as I did six or seven years ago, as for example on *Tasso*, although they are the same actors as then – that is to say, with a very strong, intensive and provocative concept with which I confronted the actors. I don't work like that any more because the actors don't want to work in this way: plunging into a passage of ten lines with seven gestures that are prescribed.

Before Stein could reach the goal he was seeking, however, there was to be one further stopping-place on the way, the Zurich Schauspielhaus.

3   Theatre structures old and new – Bond's *Early Morning* and Middleton and Rowley's *The Changeling* in Zurich, and the move to the Schaubühne, Berlin

The German-speaking nations have a radically different attitude to their theatre from that of the British or Americans. The "show-business" of the West End or Broadway, the financial deals, the long runs, the stars and the "razzmatazz" all seem to them like phantasmagoria from some capitalist nightmare, quite unrelated to art or culture. For the German it is a source of utter bewilderment that the English can buy a copy of *Hamlet* without paying tax on it, but will have 15 per cent added to the price of a ticket for watching the same play in a theatre.

The German regards his theatre as a place of enlightenment rather than of entertainment. He treats it as a library where he can enjoy the best works of world theatre, and so expects a wide variety of plays, musicals and operas. There is therefore considerable pressure on most German-language theatres to offer at least a dozen new productions each year and to present these in repertory, that is to say, with a different programme each night of the week.

In order to fulfil these expectations, the average German-language theatre has to maintain a large company, most of whose members are on two-year contracts with their city or federal state. The actors and directors are therefore municipal or state employees, with contractual guarantees and pension rights. Their salaries are negotiated on signing the contract and so they are no longer dependent on the roles they play or the public acclaim they achieve. This leads to a bureaucratic attitude in some performers, and many German productions are characterized by weary efficiency in place of theatrical excitement. As I wrote in *German theatre today:* "The British theatre may be like a prostitute selling herself on the street-corner, but she is perhaps preferable to Germany's staid matron who will often perform only from a sense of marital duty" (p. 12).

In order to run these large municipal and state theatres, a super-bureaucrat, the *Intendant,* is appointed by the authorities. He (very seldom she) is invariably a director of some experience who will continue to direct the occasional production but who will be forced to carry out many administrative duties. He is held responsible by the authorities for maintaining the quality of work in his theatre (the closest equivalent in Britain would be the Director of the National Theatre). However benevolent his attitude, it is almost inevitable that the *Intendant* will be an autocrat. The size of his operation is such that consultation is very difficult and even where structures for democratic participation supposedly exist, they are seldom very effective.

It was to such a large municipal theatre that Stein next went, and it was there at the Schauspielhaus in Zurich that Stein received final proof that even with a sympathetic *Intendant* it was impossible to work democratically within existing theatre structures. On 1 January 1969, Peter Löffler, a man of progressive views and still in his forties, had been appointed *Intendant* of the Schauspielhaus by the Zurich city council in an attempt to inject new life into a theatre that had fallen far from the pre-eminence it enjoyed during and immediately after the war.

Löffler appeared to be a reasonably safe appointment (he came from a "good" Zurich family) and no one expected his reforms to be too radical. However, he and his *Dramaturg*, Klaus Völker, a Brecht specialist, began to pursue an uncomfortably revolutionary policy and set about overhauling the repertoire of the Schauspielhaus in favour of provocative modern pieces. As part of this "overhaul" Löffler invited Stein to Zurich, where he began by directing the German première of the last play to have been banned by the British censor, Edward Bond's *Early Morning*. This extraordinary view of Queen Victoria – one of the most sacred of English cows – and of her family and political advisers contains within it all the apparent contradictions that distinguish Bond as a playwright: trenchant political analysis coupled with poetic statement, violent imagery with outrageous humour, fantastic invention with a clear historical perspective.

Stein did not in any way attempt to emasculate this monster of a play. The text remained virtually uncut, and all the episodes, especially the cannibalistic scene in heaven, were played to extract their full potential, with the result that many critics found the pacing too slow and the intensity of the playing too heavy-handed for the grotesquerie of the piece. Certainly, Charles Marowitz's production of the play the following summer in Bochum seemed to succeed much better, thanks to its pace and lightness of touch. Stein, however, was not prepared to make things easy for his audience, since it was intended as an attack on them: for Stein, cannibalism was simply a metaphor for the normal behaviour of capitalist man who devours his own kind. The violent incidents, the kicking to death of a would-be assassin or the murder and eating of a man who jumps a cinema queue, were played with heightened realism. The assassin (Tilo Prückner) was heavily padded like an ice-hockey player, so that the kicks could be more convincingly delivered, and he bit through a sac of stage blood so that the stage ran red beneath him. The skeleton of Prince George, the Siamese twin brother of Arthur, was a mummi-fied stump whose features had all but rotted away, a hideous Jaco-bean *memento mori*.

The costumes and set possessed the same degree of exaggeration. The former, designed by Susanne Raschig, ranged from parodistic versions of Victorian dress to modernistic pop-art creations. Albert, the Prince Consort, wore a tightly buttoned military uniform which later opened to reveal a swastika on his belly; Florence Nightingale combined lust with appropriate sterility by visiting the Crimean bat-tlefield wearing only a bikini and transparent plastic raincoat.

The set, built by Günter Kuschmann from designs by Uwe Lausen, was austere with the occasional grotesquely distorted property. Bas-ically an ash-grey box set with initially a reddish floor-covering, it was simply and swiftly adapted to provide the many locations of the play: a pallet for the second scene (Arthur and George in bed); for the palace in the third and fourth scenes they wheeled in Victoria's throne, as high as a tennis-umpire's seat, painted red and embel-lished with coats of arms, a kind of fantastic child's highchair. From the garden-party scene onwards, for which a green stage-cloth was revealed on the floor, a huge red and white striped deckchair, at least five times larger than normal, dominated the stage. This was used as a monument, a cave, a gallows and, sideways on, as a strangely dis-torted cross before which Arthur philosophized over the corpse of his twin brother. After the interval, heaven was represented by a now completely ash-grey set, ironically dominated by an outsize block-and-pulley and cluttered with tin cans.

In this macabre and unreal world it was to be expected that the acting style would develop the same exaggerations. The play began with the two conspirators Albert (Wolfgang Reichmann) and Disraeli (Hannes Siegl) approaching each other across an open stage as though tracing their way through a labyrinth, an image of their deviousness. Most of the lines were delivered with the intentionally rhetorical and declamatory style appropriate to Grand Guignol. Only in the modern scene, which almost seems to come from another play, where Len (Tilo Prückner) and Joyce (Ingrid Burkhard) eat the man

Fig. 3   Bond's *Early Morning*. Arthur (Bruno Ganz) philosophizes over the corpse of his Siamese twin brother.

who has annoyed them in the film queue, was the playing more natural, and the language slipped from declamation to dialect.

Of the individual performances, critics had praise for Joana Maria Gorvin (Victoria) who, though hardly of the quality of Therese Giehse, the actress originally intended for the role, maintained a dignity and credibility as Queen despite her lesbian antics with Florence Nightingale. It was Nightingale herself, played by Jutta Lampe, and Bruno Ganz, as Arthur, who gave the strongest performances. Indeed, Ganz's commitment to the role of Arthur lent it a depth and subtlety that was not wholly appropriate to the character. Bond requires of his actors not that they should "act," that is, flesh out a character from within their own resources, but that they should speak the lines with intelligence and sensitivity. In this respect he stands very close to Brecht. Jutta Lampe offered a performance which illuminated the situation without indulging in the desperate search to create a character where one hardly exists. Never superficial, she nevertheless kept near the surface of incidents. Always sensitive, she kept her emotions subdued. So she could establish a wide range of moods: having been just raped by Victoria, she staggered across the stage, her thighs painfully turned inwards like a wounded bird; offering herself to Lord Mennings, she thrust a red boot out of the long slit in her red velvet dress, every inch the whore; on the battlefield, she laid herself gently on the dying soldiers sending them to their deaths with words of love. Most extraordinary, though, was her achievement in the final scene, where she held a duologue with Arthur's severed head clenched between her thighs. What might have been laughable or distasteful was raised by the sensitivity and intelligence of the playing of Lampe and Ganz to a thing of gentle beauty. As Ivan Nagel commented (*Theater heute*, 1970/13, p. 74):

The happiness of these two is a direct product of their hopelessness, of the knowledge that the cruelty and corruption of the human race can no longer touch them, because they know that they have nothing more to gain. Almost murmuring, they exchange question and answer with flat, muted, high-pitched expressionless voices – just the occasional glance, a smile, a tiny nod of the head: understanding.

Edward Bond himself was unenthusiastic about Stein's treatment of his play, although it was this production, even more than Zadek's première of *Narrow Road to the Deep North* in Munich at the same time, that established Bond's reputation in Germany. In an interview in July 1979 Bond was asked what he thought of Stein's production. He replied (Patricia Curran, "A study of *The Woman* and an interview with its playwright Edward Bond," unpublished MA dissertation, University of Leeds, 1979, part 2, pp. 7–8):

I didn't see Stein's production, but in general I would say that German theatre is still pre-Brechtian. You can understand what Brecht was talking about when you go and see a lot of German theatre, because it's very expressionistic, very metaphysical, and you can see what he was fighting against when he wanted things to be more simple, unoperatic, direct . . . I think that [*Early Morning*] should be played for deadpan realism.

Stein's production was hardly expressionistic, but it had lost the simple directness which had so distinguished his earlier Bond production and which he was to rediscover in his later work at the Schaubühne.

A more immediate reaction to Bond's play was provided by the Zurich public themselves at the opening night on 2 October 1969. Many were already disappointed and angered by Löffler's directorship and were anyway in no mood to be generous towards a new and experimental work. Shouts and jeers greeted the announcement that one of the actors would be unable to appear because of a sprained ankle. Lines of the play remarking on how quiet it was or that it could not last much longer were greeted with hilarity and applause. Even some of the actors, notably Wolfgang Reichmann (Albert), seemed treacherously to side with the audience against the production. Seats banged noisily and doors slammed as angry theatre-goers stomped off into the night, resolved to sell their season tickets at the earliest opportunity. The scene in which the assassin was kicked to death caused such resentment amongst sections of the audience, whether from squeamishness or perhaps from understandable ire over actors playing at what some members of the audience had actually witnessed in the Third Reich, that the performance had to be interrupted. Then, during a brief lull, a lady turned to the chairman of the theatre committee on the city council and demanded to know when Zurich would once more be offered entertaining theatre ("ansprechendes Theater").

The answer came by December. The theatre committee, not one of whose members had any direct connection with the theatre, had resolved to end Löffler's contract at the end of his first season. Despite the intervention of Frisch and other writers the authorities remained adamant. Once again Stein had come face to face with the impossibility of achieving a theatre revolution within the existing structures of state and municipal theatres.

Understandably, Stein's further work in Zurich was unspectacular. *Tasso* was revived on 8 November 1969 and played for a further fourteen performances during the season, and he was called in to assist Ulrich Heising on Sean O'Casey's *Cock-a-Doodle Dandy*, which opened on 6 December 1969.

Many critics have detected Jacobean elements in the plays of Bond, and it is certainly true that the bold directing style which Stein employed for *Early Morning* was most suitable to Stein's last production in Zurich, the late Jacobean piece by Middleton and Rowley, *The Changeling*. Here too grotesque violence was juxtaposed with robust humour, here too an authoritarian structure was challenged by anarchic forces. It was these qualities that attracted the *Dramaturg* Dieter Sturm to the play, so initiating the fruitful collaboration between Sturm and Stein, which was to contribute so much to the success of the Schaubühne am Halleschen Ufer. *The Changeling* had only within the last twenty years been rediscovered for English audiences and now, on 11 June 1970, it was to have its German-language première.

The set was designed, as for *Tasso*, by Wilfried Minks. It consisted of a flat open area, seemingly composed of huge blocks of marble, the joins clearly marked by straight white lines. Sunk into this area were openings and steps, apparently leading to a network of underground passages. Around the stage was a shimmering golden wall, into which were set pale-blue neon tubes. Thus Minks's design was clean, geometric and modern, and yet captured something of the subterranean mystery of Vermandero's fortress in Alicante.

As with the opening scene of *Early Morning*, characters often followed the lines of imaginary labyrinths and stole round imaginary corners. Here too there was the same grotesquerie: stage blood in plenty, death rattles and the sadistic glee of De Flores sawing through Alonzo's finger. In the acting, Stein abandoned any attempt to make the frequent asides and violent incidents of *The Changeling* credible on a realistic level. Instead he returned to the boldly stated performances, the *plakativ* style that he had first employed in his production of *In the Jungle of Cities*. By setting the action at a distance it could be viewed as a metaphor and therefore, paradoxically, be accepted more readily than if played for realism.

Hence, to emphasize the historical context, Susanne Raschig's costumes were lavishly authentic. Bruno Ganz as De Flores did not bear any of the realistic, external ugliness that Beatrice finds so repulsive; rather he looked like a fallen angel, and his hideous features existed only in the mind of Beatrice – a product of her sexual repression. Edith Clever as Beatrice clearly signalled the stages of her descent into depravity. When, for example, Alsemero spoke to her, she first turned her head towards him, but, only after an instant, her eyes – a conscious device by the actress to indicate her duplicity.

This mannered approach, which with care and intelligence had led to such a brilliant and critical interpretation of *Tasso*, now seemed too artificial, parodistic even. Eight months later, at one of the early meetings in the Schaubühne, Stein admitted that in *The Changeling* they had "fallen on their faces" (Protocol no. 75, 10 February 1971).

While in Zurich Stein had worked with actors on a collective production of Wolfgang Deichsel's play *Frankenstein*. Though it never came to performance, it was decisive in showing Stein the possibilities of genuine group creation. In an interview in 1972 (*Spielplatz*, 1 (1972), 53–4) Bruno Ganz spoke of this

Frankenstein production, which we rehearsed for three months entirely amongst ourselves. In this context we began to consider anti-authoritarian questions like the elimination of the director etc. We were able to work without the normal pressures of getting a piece ready for performance. So of course an intensive group-feeling developed which was not necessarily political – certainly there was a political aspect to it, but initially we were something of a mutual admiration society that wanted to stay together and achieve something . . . We wanted to make the effort of working collectively, which meant that we first had to find out what that involved. People often have dogmatic views about this, just as we did at the time. We thought if each actor changed himself a little and adapted himself to the others and if the level of information were balanced out, so that where possible everyone could take equal part in the preparation, then it should actually be feasible for twenty-five people, all participating equally, to produce a play together. But that's not the way it works.

As a result of the collective work on *Frankenstein* Peter Stein and the actors (principally Ganz, Lampe and Clever) devised the so-called Zurich Paper which, like the discussions on *Tasso*, set out to define the kind of theatre within which the ensemble could "stay together and experiment with aesthetic questions and questions of organization, of the function of art in society" (interview with Zipes, *Performance* 4 (1972), 69). The three main points of the Zurich Paper were:

(1) that an "anti-capitalist" theatre should be established
(2) that the work of the theatre should be on collective lines
(3) that theatre should be fun

Stein's demand for a theatre, where the old structures and methods might be challenged and new ones tested, was answered by return-

Fig. 4 Middleton and Rowley's *The Changeling*. De Flores (Bruno Ganz), "a fallen angel," approaches Beatrice (Edith Clever) across the maze-like set.

ing to the scene of his débâcle in January 1969, the Schaubühne am
Halleschen Ufer in West Berlin. While working at the Kammerspiele
Stein had already shown an interest in the Schaubühne. His friend,
the Bavarian actress Ruth Drexel, had performed there, and Wolfgang Schwiedrzik, his co-director on the *Vietnam-Discourse*, had
directed there.

The Schaubühne am Halleschen Ufer had been created in 1962 by
Berlin students with an interest in pursuing theatre outside the conventional pattern of subsidized municipal theatres on the one hand
and commercial places of light entertainment on the other. The two
Gesellschafter or licensees of the undertaking, Jürgen Schitthelm, a
director, and Klaus Weiffenbach, a set-designer, entered into nego-
tiations with a West Berlin trade union and were given the lease on
a hall in a fairly run-down area of the city some distance from the
centre of Berlin's theatre and entertainment centre. Here they presented simple stagings of largely experimental and left-wing plays
(the 1969–70 programme contained three plays by Brecht and one by
Horváth), presented *ensuite* instead of in rotation, which is the usual
repertory system of municipal theatres. From the outset emphasis
was placed on collective work, and all full-time members of the theatre were paid the same wages.

In the wake of the anti-authoritarian swing in German politics,
signalled by the replacement of Adenauer's Christian Democrats by
Brandt's Social Democrat government and, more dramatically, by the
student riots of 1967–8, participation or "co-determination" (*Mitbes-
timmung*) had become a recurrent demand, especially in industry and
education. Even more than in industry, however, participation in
the theatre may be expected to affect directly the quality of the product. It will not necessarily make for a better screw if a lathe-operator
has a voice in management decisions, but an actor who has been
consulted about the way a play is rehearsed and has agreed to the
decisions affecting the production will undoubtedly give a better
performance than one who is merely doing as he is told. As Stein
said on 4 September 1970 (interview in *Christ und Welt*): "When people on stage know what they want to communicate, their performances will gain tremendously in conviction."

It was remarkable that the call for Stein to found a theatre on socialist lines eventually came from the politically most sensitive area of
West Germany, the city of West Berlin. But the reasons were not hard
to find. Ever since the final division of Berlin, politically in 1948 and
physically, with the building of the Wall, in 1961, the West Berlin
Senate had spent vast subsidies from the Federal Republic in order

to maintain the economic viability of the city and to make it a show-case of Western achievement in the midst of East German territory.

There were many ways of achieving this, but one relatively cheap method was to raise the standard of cultural life in the old capital. So the municipal theatres of West Berlin regularly received subsidies at least half as high again as those common to other major cities, and the opera house was the most generously supported theatre in the whole of Germany, receiving a grant approximately equivalent to the Arts Council annual subsidy to all British theatres. But money alone does not guarantee quality.

Characteristic of the general cultural stagnation was Boleslaw Barlog, the long-standing *Intendant* of the Berlin municipal theatres. He was an authoritarian of the old school, who refused to perform Brecht after the erection of the Berlin Wall in 1961, who called in police to defend the Schillertheater with batons and pistols when in 1968 students tried to interrupt a performance to initiate a political discussion. He threatened any member of the audience who booed with either banishment from the theatre or even prosecution for causing a disturbance of the peace. He dismissed a painter because he had held a small Christmas party in the paintshop, and yet insisted that theatre technicians should restore some of his antiques.

Moreover, the repertoires of the Barlog theatres were unadventurous: in the years leading up to 1969 there had been no Ibsen, Strindberg, Schnitzler, Synge, Pirandello, O'Neill, Sartre, Georg Kaiser, Gatti or Dürrenmatt. Despite the successful première of Peter Weiss's *Marat/Sade* at the Schillertheater, he was no longer performed because his plays had become too overtly political. "'Kids' theatre is a load of crap, if you'll forgive the expression," said Barlog on Berlin radio on 3 May 1970 and included Stein amongst the "kids." A year later he was recorded as saying, *Theaterrundschau*, 5 (1971): "What I like is the theatre of the good old days." He was rewarded by an aging audience, whose numbers were gradually declining. When asked by the Berlin newspaper *Der Abend* (24 April 1969) how he explained the growing unpopularity of his theatres, Barlog blamed the hostile attitude of the critics, the effects of television, but above all the "spiritual smugness" of the public: "It will take care of itself in time. When people are worse off again, they will seek a spiritual experience and their love for the church and the theatre will awake once more."

The West Berlin Senator for Culture, fortuitously also named Stein, was not prepared to wait for Barlog's spiritual revival, and on the advice of a young civil servant, Wolfgang Nürmberger, set about

wooing Stein and his actors for Berlin. After all, the dozen or so theatres of West Berlin had failed to produce a single production worthy
of inclusion in the 1970 Berlin Festival, whereas two of Stein's productions had been invited (*Tasso* and *Early Morning*). The 1.8 million
DM (£225,000), which was to be the initial annual subsidy to the new
Schaubühne, and which represented 72 per cent of the total budget,
was a cheap price to pay for attracting the most outstanding German
theatre ensemble to West Berlin.

For Stein, it represented the opportunity at last to establish a working situation where serious theatrical exploration might take place.
Stein's primary consideration was ever the immediate and practical
demands of his work in the theatre rather than some detached political philosophy. By now he was an informed Marxist, and it seemed
evident that the best theatre creation could be achieved only within
a co-operative and democratic structure, not in the competitive and
authoritarian structure of the traditional municipal theatre. In 1968
Stein had already stated (*Theater heute*, 1968/13, p. 29):

I cannot separate my work from the institution in the way that, for example,
Zadek does – and does with great success. I find it necessary to consider how
the organization of this institution can be changed . . . I have discovered
that a change, a restructuring of existing institutions isn't possible. It is quite
impossible because these institutions are inseparable from the bureaucratic
effects and organizational pressures of those who provide the money. There
is the possibility of individual initiative within the capitalist system to find
money that is free from the values and strictures of the bureaucracy, as much
money as possible, with which a theatre can be founded, where people who
need to leave the existing institutions can come together. But of course that's
terribly hard.

Now Stein had found his money and was at last able to create the
kind of institution in which he could discover with certain people
"what you can actually do with theatre." He has never regarded this
as part of a specific political programme and he has grown increas-
ingly wary of the label "model" being attached to the Schaubühne.
This is worth remembering when accusations are made that Stein
has betrayed the early political idealism of his theatre. As he said on
21 July 1977 (*Der Abend*): "Nowhere on earth is there a democracy
which functions in complete purity; why does everyone expect it to
happen here?" He has been consistently pragmatic in supporting
any decision that permits a valuable, thoughtful and committed theatre to thrive – even at the expense of compromising formal democratic procedures. Doing precedes dogma.

The breach between the Schaubühne's two licensees and Stein
over the *Vietnam-Discourse* was quickly closed, and the initial annual

subsidy of 1.8 million DM (more than three times that of the previous year) was agreed with the Senate. A *Direktorium* (management committee) was set up, consisting of the two licensees, Schitthelm and Weiffenbach, as permanent appointments, together with three other members elected by a general meeting of the whole theatre staff. Initially, the three were Stein, Claus Peymann and Dieter Sturm.

While the function of the *Direktorium* was to take day-to-day decisions, ultimate authority lay in the *Vollversammlung* (general meeting). It was to meet once a month (more frequently if a third of the staff agreed) and could veto any decisions taken by the "management." In order to permit even more effective channels of communication, a further subcommittee called a *Gremium* was set up. This consisted of two representatives each from the actors and the technicians, and one each from the administration and the production staff (i.e. directors, designers, *Dramaturgen* (etc.). The *Gremium* met the *Direktorium* twice a week to represent the interests of the membership and to report back to the appropriate body. The distinction between actors and production staff was not an ideal arrangement but was dictated by the practical consideration that the production staff could meet in the evenings while the actors were performing on stage. Meetings between the two groups were anyway frequent.

Proper participation in decision-making could only take place if there were free access to information at all levels. It became therefore an essential element of this exercise in democracy that precise "Protocols" were recorded and rapidly circulated, and there was a permanent member of staff who had sole responsibility for this task.

The levels of wages were considerably modified to counter the star-system, whereby a top actor could earn eight times more than his junior colleagues. The minimum was now set at 1,000 DM per month (£1,500 per annum) and the maximum at 2,700 DM (£4,000 per annum). Technicians, who, unlike the actors, were paid for any overtime over the eight hours prescribed by their unions, received the agreed union rate, giving them on average a basic wage of less than 1,000 DM (£1,500 per annum). In order to give the ensemble continuity, actors' contracts (with the licensees, not, as is usual, with the town council) were generally for two years.

Participation was also sought in the appointment of new staff, and a committee was formed consisting of the two directors and several actors to make recommendations to the *Direktorium*, especially in the light of casting needs.

Finally, seminars of political instruction were instituted for all employees of the theatre. Predictably, the main topic was to be Marxism and the classes were "to contribute to the establishment of a consensus of political and artistic opinion as the basis of a true working ensemble" (Stein at a press conference, 14 December 1970, quoted in Sandmeyer, p. 109).

Once established, the structure of the Schaubühne functioned remarkably well, not only creating work of the highest standard but also showing the rest of Germany and the world the possibilities of

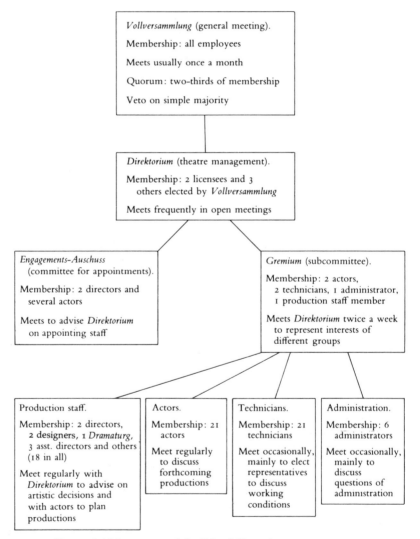

Fig. 5   Initial structure of the Schaubühne, August 1970.

a truly democratic theatre organization. Here was no hippy commune like the Living Theatre nor a political group churning out dismal propaganda, but an extremely thoughtful, self-critical, hard-working and hard-headed collection of people dedicated to pursuing experiments in theatre, not as a masturbatory aesthetic exercise but as a serious investigation of society using theatrical means.

Regrettably, however, the Schaubühne was threatened by three enemies: those outside who hoped to see this left-wing enterprise fail, those within who wished to use the Schaubühne's experiment in democracy as a political platform rather than as a more effective means of creating political theatre, and – simply – time.

The attack from outside came from the Christian Democrat Unionists in the Senate. Horrified that the new Schaubühne had opened with the overtly revolutionary play, Brecht's *The Mother*, shocked to learn of the regular seminars held on the theories of Marx and Lenin, the CDU, armed with Protocols stolen from the theatre, proposed a Senate motion to block all subsidies to the Schaubühne on the grounds that it "pursues Communist infiltration and has acted contrary to the Constitution" (Debate of 10 December 1970).

The Schaubühne mentor, the Senator for Culture, Professor Werner Stein, rejected this motion on grounds of artistic freedom, but the CDU further claimed that the accounts of the Schaubühne were not in order and insisted that productions should be costed in advance (an impossibility, since the whole point of the Schaubühne method was that decisions were taken by everyone involved in the work process and so nothing could be laid down in advance).

The CDU faction were supported by a number of *Sozialdemokratische Partei Deutschlands* (*SPD*) senators, and the subsidies were blocked. The Schaubühne seemed doomed within four months of its founding, and seventeen eminent theatre critics wrote an open letter of protest to the Mayor of West Berlin. After examining all the Protocols and accounts, the Senate finally established that there was nothing in the work of the Schaubühne which was "anti-constitutional" and the subsidies were restored. This was a victory for the theatre, but the paradoxical situation was inescapable: this ensemble, committed to revolutionary political thinking, could be made financially viable only if their activities were accounted politically ineffectual.

There have been recurrent crises over the level of subsidies and, more recently, the financing of a new theatre-building, the Mendelssohn-Bau. By November 1974 the Schaubühne was in serious financial difficulties with 1 million DM (£150,000) in debts. The Senate came to the rescue but the following year granted only 5½ million DM (£920,000) instead of the demanded 6,900,000 DM (£1,200,000). Stein threatened to go to another city, and this was sufficient to cause the Senate to agree to the building of a new theatre (24 October 1975), the cost of which has subsequently risen to something in the region of 100 million DM (£25 million). From being a cheap investment, the Schaubühne now is one of the best endowed theatre companies in the world, its annual subsidy now standing at over eight million DM (£2 million).

The second initial threat to the Schaubühne came from within. Most of the team Stein gathered around him were intensely loyal to him personally and very committed to the concept of the Schaubühne. He had brought with him, from Munich, Michael König Dieter Laser and the designer Karl-Ernst Herrmann, from Bremen, the core of his acting ensemble, Jutta Lampe, Bruno Ganz, Edith Clever, Werner Rehm and Sabine Andreas, and from Zurich, Tilo Prückner and the costume-designer Susanne Raschig. Others, like Otto Sander and the *Dramaturg* Dieter Sturm, who were part of the original Schaubühne company, had already worked with Stein. However, there were members of the Schaubühne, especially amongst the technicians, who resented Stein's pervasive influence and the devotion of the actors to him. To this day, on the stairway leading up to the lighting-box, one can see in large red letters: "STEIN IST DOOF" ("Stein is daft").

There were recurrent problems with technicians. Some were not trained technicians at all but sought employment at the renowned Schaubühne in the hope of moving into more artistic areas. It is, for example, not uncommon for the theatre porter to be writing a doctorate or composing a symphony. This has often led to resentment by those who felt their talents were being wasted.

Moreover, union rules did not permit technicians to work for more than eight hours a day without receiving overtime. Their basic rate of pay was correspondingly lower than that of actors who often put in a fourteen or sixteen hour day. The lower pay and menial tasks of the technicians made them appear underprivileged, and the actors sometimes rather sentimentally supported their protests, even when the technicians were clearly in the wrong (unpunctuality, incompetent work etc.). "The class-war was being fought in our own theatre," as Stein wryly remarked to Bergmann. There was constant friction between the directors and the technicians, who, after all, had an equal say with the actors in the choice of play in which the actors would appear nightly. In April 1972 things came to a head when the

Vollversammlung used its veto for the first time to block a *Direktorium* decision to sack a technician. Stein immediately resigned from the *Direktorium* and agreed to stand for re-election only after the *Vollversammlung* had passed a resolution on 6 May that those on short-term contracts should no longer have the right of veto. This ruling, which principally affected technicians and front-of-house staff, was greeted with jubilation by the right-wing press of Berlin, producing headlines like: "Schaubühne: the end of participation!"

In fact, participation did not end but was made much more practicable – on lines that are now common to all major institutions and firms in West Germany. Here the third factor, time, became important. The Schaubühne had wisely resisted the pressures on municipal theatres to mount an annual repertory of some dozen plays by committing themselves to only four productions a year (250 performances). It could therefore approach each project with time and care. Nevertheless, despite the untiring commitment shown by Stein and the actors, the added burden of regular meetings and the seemingly endless flow of duplicated Protocols eventually proved unbearable. Since the middle of 1972 the interests of the technicians have been represented by a *Betriebsrat* (works committee) and the *Vollversammlung* now meets only twice a year with no power of veto. By January 1973, too, the political seminars were finally suspended, and only Protocols concerned with specific production issues were distributed after 1975. To some extent, the experiment in full-scale participation had failed: there was not always the good will, there certainly was not the time. What has remained, though, is the most valuable aspect of the attempt: the practice of involving all participants in the decisions affecting a production, so that actors are consulted about casting, design, overall conception and so on. As we shall see, this form of participation depends on a willingness to question and be questioned at each stage of the rehearsal process. Where such willingness exists, the results can be staggeringly impressive.

4   Theatre of revolution – Brecht's
     The Mother, Workers' Theatre and
     Vishnevsky's *Optimistic Tragedy*

For the sake of convenience and perhaps as an acknowledgment of one of the major impulses towards the founding of the new Schaubühne, the theatre opened on 27 August 1970 with a further revival of *Tasso*. Excitement however centred on the theatre's first collective production, which was to express the socialist convictions of the company. As Stein recorded in an interview with Bernard Dort (*Travail théâtral*, 1972, pp. 19–20):

We wanted to concern ourselves with topics that are not normally treated in the theatre, to study the history of revolution or revolutions and the history of the workers' movement. That was our firm intention. And we were aware of all that that implies: developing political consciousness, studying historical fact, etc., in short, the need for us to make discoveries not only in the aesthetic field but also, and above all, in historical matters. And that takes a lot of time.

The play chosen for this initial study of revolution was Brecht's *Die Mutter (The Mother),* written in 1931 and premièred in Berlin in 1932 with Helene Weigel in the title-role. Ideally, of course, the play should have been chosen by collective decision, but Stein justifiably felt it important for the ensemble (and for sceptical outsiders) that work should commence as soon as possible. He justified the choice of play on three grounds (press conference, 11 May 1970):

First, the subject of the play is of interest – the pre-history of the October Revolution in Russia. Secondly, it is of interest because Brecht wrote it as a *Lehrstück; Lehrstück* represents a learning process for those who take part in it . . . A third point is that as part of this learning process we hope to benefit a great deal from the involvement of Frau Giehse [the actress playing the Mother].

In fact, rehearsals began just two days after the inception of the new Schaubühne – on 3 August 1970. Nine hours of daily rehearsal were the norm, usually from 10 a.m. to 3 p.m. and from 7 p.m. to 11 p.m. In order to emphasize the collective nature of the undertaking, it was required of all actors that they should attend every rehearsal. Discussions were held at the conclusion of each rehearsal, and three fuller discussions ("rehearsal criticisms") were arranged and their minutes distributed to the administration and technicians. There

46

was a "collective" of three directors, Stein himself, Wolfgang Schwiedrzik and Frank-Patrick Steckel. Their function was to implement the collective decisions of the ensemble. Stein described the division of their responsibilities as follows (*Frankfurter Neue Presse*, 3 October 1970): "Steckel did most of the preparatory work. We all three conduct the rehearsals; I make the final proposals to the actors." Of particular value was the constant presence of the *Dramaturg* Dieter Sturm at rehearsals. In most German theatres the *Dramaturg* is seldom very involved in the actual rehearsal process, but Sturm is an especially committed *Dramaturg*, for whom Stein has nothing but praise: "Without Sturm the Schaubühne would be nothing . . . [He] sets the tone, I just get things moving" (*Travail théâtral*, 1972, p. 23), "Sturm is the real soul of this theatre" (unpublished interview with Bergmann, 1978). During work on *The Mother* his consistently well-informed and critical attitude helped greatly in shaping the course of the production.

On the negative side, there were again problems of time. Actors felt frustrated at being made to sit through rehearsals when they were not required for a scene, especially as they carried the added burden of participating in the running of the theatre. With a cast of twenty-two, not to mention all the other participants like the musical director and costume-designers, it was clearly impossible for everyone to contribute satisfactorily to the rehearsals and discussions, and the pre-eminence of the directors became established as a course of necessity. Eventually, after dissatisfaction had been voiced, particularly at the third full discussion on 10 September, the obligation to attend rehearsals was lifted.

The play itself also presented problems. Based on a novel by Gorky, *The Mother* traces the development of political consciousness in the central figure, Pelagea Wlassowa, from her distrust of the political activities of her son to her active participation in political agitation leading to the October Revolution in 1917. Brecht had written the piece to be performed before the workers of Berlin in 1932 in an attempt to mobilize the proletariat against the forces of Fascism. Its intention was unashamedly propagandistic, and it presented an abstract, idealized situation, which some members of the Schaubühne ensemble initially found "like something from a fairy-tale" and "too beautiful to be true." As Stein said in an interview (*BZ*, Berlin, 18 January 1971):

We are agreed that we cannot employ the kind of agitation that was common in the twenties when there was a great revolutionary political party. For us agitation means simply endeavouring to affect the consciousness of those who come to our theatre in such a way that social change and socialist change can at least become topics for discussion.

The political situation had changed from that of the early thirties, and the audience of the Schaubühne were quite different from Brecht's. There was, however, no misguided attempt to make the play more topical by blurring its historical situation; nor was there any desire to present the piece as a quaint example of Brechtiana without any contemporary relevance (although some critics did precisely that in their reviews).

Initially the actors had difficulty in relating to each other as a group of workers in the early years of this century. Part of the problem lay in the fact that Brecht treats the party comrades as a given element of the story; he makes no attempt to establish their background or explain how they have come together. At this point a good British or American director would no doubt begin to suggest improvisation as a means for the actors to create a more tangible world for themselves. Characteristically, however, the Schaubühne actors were encouraged to go off and steep themselves in revolutionary literature in order to raise their political consciousness (and this in addition to nine hours' rehearsal per day plus frequent meetings!). As Stein said of his actors (*Travail théâtral*, 1972, p. 28): "They prepare themselves intensively for productions in a way that one might call cerebral. It's essential: it's a question of knowing what you're doing."

For the set Klaus Weiffenbach removed the usual proscenium stage of the Schaubühne and replaced it with a large flat thrust. The audience sat on three sides and the ensemble sat across the back, remaining visible throughout, adding to the concentration of the performance, stepping forward to help with set-changes or to take part in the action. For many actors, it was their first experience of exposing themselves in this way, and it was a great help in acquiring the necessary techniques that at the early rehearsals the benches at the sides could be filled with fellow actors. For the audience, the seating arrangement reinforced the critical attitude they were invited to adopt: the action was not seen from one point of view only but, as in a boxing-match, each spectator could assess events "from his angle." On the other hand, because some two-thirds of the spectators were visible to each member of the audience, one had the sense of sharing in a communal response, as though participating in a tribunal called in to pass judgment on what was shown on stage. Finally, the open staging, like the brilliant white lighting throughout, robbed the performance of any "magic of the theatre" – there were no special effects, no dramatic entrances, no sudden lighting-changes, simply a story told clearly and efficiently.

Apart from the panel above the stage, carrying the captions, and screens to the left and right for projections, there was very little in the way of setting: minimal furniture for the interior scenes, a red flag for the demonstrations, a single free-standing grating to represent the prison. The set design was used ingeniously to represent a development in the consciousness of the characters. Thus, in comparison with the austere furnishings of Pelagea Wlassowa's home, the room of the *petit bourgeois* Teacher seemed quite elegant: a row of stage flats with thin striped wallpaper, adorned with a portrait of the Czar, upholstered dining chairs and a fine carved table covered with a lace cloth. As the Teacher gradually became drawn into the Revolution and the reality of the world outside penetrated his life, so the symbols of bourgeois prosperity and enclosure were gradually dismantled: the flats were removed, the cloth was whisked away, and the table now served as a base for the press for printing revolutionary leaflets.

The search for an appropriate acting style for the piece provided one of the greatest challenges. The workers, frequently unnamed, could and indeed should be played in Brecht's "epic" style, presenting and not becoming a character, directing attention to the general situation of a scene and not seeking prominence for their individual parts in it. As Stein himself put it (Protocol of third full rehearsal discussion, 10 September 1970):

one ought to perform in such a way as to describe the situation of a person or a group. This is an eminently theatrical process. If, for example, a child plays at Fathers and Mothers, this is a tremendously theatrical process, but it will never lose sight of the fact that the child is simply communicating: I am Father. This in itself is the reason why it is such fun.

There are characters in the play, however, that need more "fleshing out" than the simple communication "I am Fourth Worker" will permit. An obvious example is the main character, Pelagea Wlassowa. Much nonsense has been written about Brecht's supposed insistence that the audience should not develop empathy for his characters. Brecht would hardly have troubled to write plays about people with whom it was impossible to empathize. What he did object to was an uncritical empathy towards his characters. When Mother Courage obstinately trundles her cart off in search of further profit, one should be moved by her predicament but equally angry at her stupidity and even angrier at a world that offers her no choice

other than to behave stupidly. The same is true of "Mother" Wlassowa, although she is a more positive figure than Mother Courage,
a figure who finds a way out of the contradictions in which she finds
herself.

To play the part of Wlassowa, Stein had engaged Therese Giehse,
who had worked with Brecht before the war and whom Brecht once
described as "the finest actress in Europe." Stein had got to know
her in 1965 in his early days at the Munich Kammerspiele during
rehearsals for Gerd Hofmann's *Der Sohn* (*The Son*). As a young
Regieassistent, Stein was surprised and gratified that Giehse was the
first actress or actor to pay any attention to his comments. Stein
claimed to have learned more from her about Brecht than from any
other source.

To the part of Wlassowa Giehse brought a reticence of style and an
attention to detail that would have been the pride of a Stanislavskian
actress. But the function of accurately observed detail was here motivated by quite different considerations from those of the naturalistic
performer. The latter would use detail to render the character more
realistic, to make the illusion more credible; Giehse used it to make
Wlassowa more *real,* not creating the illusion of being the character
but showing how a mother in Wlassowa's situation would really
behave. In the fifth scene, for example, where Wlassowa "receives
her first lesson in political economy," she was invited by two of the
workers to discuss the forthcoming strike. Giehse sat down between
them on the couch, her hands clasped firmly in her lap as a sign that
she would not easily be swayed by their arguments. Her brow fur-
rowed, her lips pursed, she quickly responded with a certain smugness: I own this table, so I can do with it what I like; Suchlinow owns
the factory, so why can't he do with it what he likes? Gradually, as
the arguments of the workers won her over, the suspicious tension
in her body relaxed, her gestures became freer, she became one with
the young revolutionaries.

In the tenth scene, where her son Pawel (Heinrich Giskes) has
escaped from prison and must leave at once for Moscow under party
orders, Giehse quickly and silently fetched his greatcoat, helped him
into it, stood hidden behind him for a moment with just her hands
visible clutching his upper arms. She then quickly released her grip
and pushed him away. The love and sacrifice of a mother were communicated by the simplest means. Volker Canaris summarized
Giehse's performance as follows (*Die Mutter. Regiebuch der
Schaubühnen-Inszenierung,* p. 117):

Therese Giehse presents Wlassowa as a very human figure, good-humoured and sulky, good-natured and angry, weary and active. This Mother remains from first to last a proletarian, but her behaviour changes (and the production demonstrates this growth of consciousness as a practical not as a psychological process): her humanity becomes revolutionary, her good nature turns to supporting her fellow workers, from being a mother she becomes the Mother of the Revolution.

While the proletarian figures could be performed in Brecht's epic, demonstrational style, and the genius of Therese Giehse made possible a rounded characterization that still succeeded in concentrating on social and not psychological truths, the ensemble felt that these

4 Brecht's *The Mother*. Scene 3: Pelagea Wlassowa (Therese Giehse) resolves to help the revolutionary workers by smuggling leaflets into the factory.

possibilities were not suitable for the bourgeois figures in the piece. As with the more naturalistic setting of the Teacher's room, it was argued that a more conventional and individualized style of performance was more appropriate to characters like the Commissar or the Landlady. Thus, the outmoded self-indulgence of the bourgeoisie could be reflected in the emotive style of their acting and could be contrasted with the quiet self-effacing manner of the proletariat.

The most striking example of this ideological contrast of acting styles was provided by Günter Lampe as the Teacher. To quote Canaris again (*ibid.*, pp. 110–11):

> At first Lampe performs with as much artistry and perfection as Clever: with one hand on his back under his coat-flaps he parades up and down, teaching the workers; with his other hand he beats in time with his speeches, adjusts his spectacles, writes daintily with the chalk. With precise emphasis, somewhat superciliously he instructs his grown-up pupils, he pedantically corrects the way they hold their pencils . . . Lampe presents the Teacher as what one normally calls a "rounded character."
>
> But in the same way that the Teacher goes through a learning process, just as he is forced to readjust his social attitude in the course of the play, so Lampe conceals his acting more and more. His performance gradually becomes simpler and less obvious, until you hardly notice how he finally goes to the printing press quietly and unobtrusively to take out the leaflets. Lampe describes the dismantling of a typically bourgeois attitude through the dismantling of typically bourgeois acting techniques: the performer bursting with his own virtuosity becomes an economical and precisely functioning part of a collective . . . In this way the production exploits the aesthetic expectations of the bourgeois audience, whose consciousness is the same as that of the Teacher at the beginning – but then upsets those expectations in order to challenge their consciousness.

How much the consciousness of the bourgeois audience was challenged, it is impossible to tell. According to their own political viewpoint, critics regarded the production as a tremendous success or as a well-performed but outmoded piece of political propaganda. Hellmuth Karasek, writing in *Die Zeit* (16 October 1970), rather patronizingly spoke of the "defiance" of the production which reminded him of a Salvation Army band bravely singing in front of a supermarket, and Peter Iden (cf. *Die Schaubühne*, p. 37), on seeing the Mayor of West Berlin giving a standing ovation, was reminded of the bourgeois audiences of Piscator's theatre enthusiastically applauding those who were intent on destroying the power of the bourgeoisie.

Despite the political act of attempting to alter the consciousness of the bourgeoisie, many members of the Schaubühne felt it essential that their work should also be directed at the workers in whose name they were making theatre. So it was that special performances of *The Mother* were laid on, to which only apprentices and young workers (ultimately some 3,000) were invited. Response to the production varied, but Stein (Protocol of evaluation of *The Mother* production, 14 October 1970) had to admit that there was not much interest shown in it when it was first performed to apprentices of *IG Metall*. He wondered whether this was due to the apprentices, the play or the production. As Sandmeyer points out (p. 125), it was not surprising that the subtle conception as reflected by Günter Lampe's playing, a conception which depended on the bourgeois sophistication of the regular theatre-goer, would be lost on young workers. Thereafter the ensemble adapted its performance, presenting only the first five scenes, playing faster and with broader strokes, when acting before a proletarian audience (six such performances were given in outside locations, on one occasion to an audience of two thousand).

But this was only a makeshift and the decision was soon taken (on 24 November 1970) to found a "Workers' and Apprentices' Theatre," which would cater for their specific needs. A "project group" was set up for this, with a new member of the production staff, a Swiss politician by the name of Franz Rueb, as co-ordinator. The main decisions of this group were that forthcoming productions should be specially designed for a workers' audience, that they should be taken to places where workers regularly met instead of attempting to bring proletarian audiences into the theatre itself, and, above all, that political argument should be placed before aesthetic considerations. As Stein explained to Bernard Dort (*Travail théâtral*, 1972, p. 24):

It was never our intention to create a popular theatre, but we should like gradually to reach another audience, by other means – without immediately having too many illusions about it. So what we intend to explore, within the context of such a workers' theatre, is a form of theatre where the audience are ultimately the ones who create the theatre – we don't intend to introduce more or less false participation but hope that what is shown will directly concern the audience and involve them in debate, indeed make them question their own way of debating.

Post-performance discussions were therefore from the outset regarded as essential and often lasted longer than the performance itself. Both in rehearsals and discussions certain difficulties rapidly came to the fore. One of these was the recurrent difficulty of finding the appropriate theatrical means. With its bourgeois audiences the Schaubühne was dealing with more or less known tastes and expectations regarding the theatre. With its proletarian audiences there was no such background and therefore no possibility of exploiting their expectations, as had been done with the regular audiences of *The Mother*. As Franz Rueb was forced to confess two years later (*Kürbiskern*, 2 (April 1973), 339):

If you have some knowledge of the history of theatrical experiment in or for the working classes, then you can see that it has only ever reached a level of communication, breadth and quality within the class struggle, when the working classes themselves were actively involved in it. And without this dimension it is difficult to get very far. You can progress step by step, that is clear, but it is impossible to achieve something that is really new and of great quality in this direction.

And *Theater heute*, (1973/13, p. 43) quoted Rueb as admitting that the value of the Workers' Theatre lay more in offering the actors an opportunity to develop than in politicizing the audience.

Apart from *The Mother*, the only other production to be transferred from the theatre to be performed to young workers (and then only on three occasions) was Hans-Magnus Enzensberger's *Das Verhör von Habana* (*The Havana Hearing*), which opened on 2 February 1971. This was the first truly collective production of the Schaubühne, involving those who were not working on Claus Peymann's production of Peter Handke's *Der Ritt über den Bodensee* (*The Ride Across Lake Constance*). For this piece, based on transcripts from the trial of Cuban exiles captured after the abortive Bay of Pigs invasion in 1961, Stein therefore found himself acting on stage and contributing as an equal to the production.

Initially, rehearsals were conducted by a different "director" every two days, which offered the ensemble plenty of time for discussion and exploration. Towards the end, however, each of the six individual hearings was allocated to a different director. Predictably, this led to a certain unevenness in presentation and a lack of a clear overall conception. Not through any arrogance, but because he remained unconvinced by this method of working, Stein was unhappy with this project and was repeatedly late for rehearsals.

The production was found to be generally boring and played to small houses with resultant financial loss. Its greatest contribution was to help the young ensemble to define the limitations of participation in collective productions. At the meeting of artistic staff and actors on 11 February 1971, three proposals were made for future collective work. The first came from Stein, who insisted that a clearer conception should be developed initially. When directing himself, he resisted having a too clearly defined original conception, but thought that, where so many people were participating, agreement

would have to be reached early, otherwise rehearsals would be interrupted by endless discussions about basic approach. Secondly,
Schwiedrzik proposed the establishment of a "collective leadership"
who would conduct rehearsals. Thirdly, it was agreed that future collective productions should be shown to other members of the theatre
two weeks in advance of the opening night, so that criticism and
suggestions might be made.

Meanwhile, on 6 February 1971 in a youth club in Essen, Stein had
premièred the first of the pieces specifically prepared for the Workers' and Apprentices' Theatre. This was Gerhard Kelling's *Die
Auseinandersetzung* (*The Altercation* or *The Reckoning*), an hour-long
piece, which Stein had rehearsed with seven of the Schaubühne
actors (Michael König amongst them) in a mere two weeks. The play
is a documentary piece based on events surrounding a strike at an
ironworks in Bremen in 1968. In the ensuing settlement with the
union, the activist shop steward responsible for the strike was dismissed from the factory and sacked from the union. Without opening
up wider ideological issues Kelling's play gives a sober account of
the perennial gap between union leadership and those on the shop
floor, a subject of immediate relevance to the young workers for
whom the production was designed.

With such a short rehearsal period and in the dubious belief that
any political theatre for such audiences must in itself be progressive
(cf. Protocol of discussion on Apprentices' Theatre, 29 November
1970), Stein's direction of *The Altercation* was unadventurous. The
acting relied on shorthand characterization of the different roles and,
necessarily for a touring production, the sets were simple. Above all,
the thinly written documentary style of the piece allowed little
opportunity for exploration. As Stein said in 1973: "We were soon
finished with *The Altercation* because the content is so meagre, as is
the form. You soon arrive at the point where you say you can't fully
and productively identify with it. And as soon as the sources of
enthusiasm and theatricality recede, you begin to lose interest in it"
(*Kürbiskern*, 2 (April 1973), 338).

To add to their difficulties, Stein and his actors found themselves
subject to a ban imposed by the leadership of several trade unions.
This was a result in part of the critical attitude to the unions adopted
by the ensemble in post-performance discussions of *The Mother* but
also more obviously because of the controversial subject matter of
The Altercation. This meant that, apart from one performance to the
Socialist Unity Party of West Germany and one to post office apprentices during the Frankfurt Theatre Festival, all the other twenty-five

performances were performed to randomly composed parties in youth clubs and the like, and not to homogeneous groups of young workers and apprentices, since union premises could not be used. The major drawback with performing in youth clubs (price of admission about 3 DM – then about 50p) was that local students, sixth-formers and political activists were attracted by the name of the Schaubühne and would dominate subsequent discussions from a primarily intellectual standpoint. Nevertheless, the Schaubühne persevered with this work, sending out some of the finest actors in German theatre at a considerable financial loss to perform to audiences that often totalled less than fifty.

In retrospect Stein now regards this Workers' and Apprentices' Theatre as peripheral to his main concern which is to create good theatre as a political act. The Workers' Theatre was neither good theatre nor did it have any demonstrable political impact. In an interview with Rudolf Bergmann (1978, unpublished) Stein recalled the most successful performance of *The Havana Hearing*, when it was played to two thousand students holding a sit-in at West Berlin's Technical University: "It was a tremendous get-together . . . It wasn't us who were performing, but the students – they were the most important actors . . . It really had nothing to do with theatre . . . I might just as well have put up posters or strummed a guitar, I could have simply read out a text." It soon became clear that theatre was but one of the means, and not necessarily an especially good one, to effect political change. For those with no particularly strong political awareness there existed better ways of being converted to a revolutionary consciousness. For those who were committed to a political cause, like the students at the Technical University, the theatrical experience could be exchanged for any other.

The particular strength of Stein and his ensemble was in creating a theatre that explored aspects of human existence, above all, social and political aspects, in a way that could not be achieved by any other process. So Stein returned to what he regarded as the proper concern of theatre and – after his involvement in *The Havana Hearing* and his direction of *The Altercation* – never again directly took part in the Workers' and Apprentices' Theatre. As he said at a meeting on 17 November 1975 (Protocol no. 499):

The introduction of the concept of specific group theatre [*Zielgruppentheater*] was a polemical exercise. We said we wouldn't perform for people like us but for others. Grown-ups will do children's theatre. Or people who have never stood at a work-bench, will presume to communicate certain important things to workers, in a neat cultural package. We now prefer to say that we will organize performances for ourselves, that people who are not like us may participate in them and profit by them. This is the conclusion we have come to.

In fact, in common with all other West German theatres, and indeed with most socialist theatre groups in the Western world, the Schaubühne has failed to win a significantly proletarian element for its audience despite the fact that it is situated in a working-class area of the city. Stein's optimistic hope that workers might learn to participate in the experience of bourgeois theatre has not been realized. But the present stance of the Schaubühne is undoubtedly more honest than its earlier pretence at creating a Workers' Theatre. Moreover, its actors have thereby been able to concentrate more on what they can do best and have been able to leave Workers' Theatre and Children's Theatre to groups specializing in these areas (Theatermanufaktur, Grips, Rote Grütze, etc.).

This did not mean, of course, that after Kelling's *The Altercation* Stein lost his interest in producing political plays. Indeed, his next project was to mount a piece dealing with the Paris Commune. Unfortunately, this idea was never realized. As Stein explained to Jack Zipes: "This was due to the fear of creating something that did not have a set text, one of my big fears. [He had considered and rejected Brecht's *Days of the Commune* and Adamov's *Spring 71*]. With Dieter [Sturm] this loomed big too, because he has programmed his mind to think that he cannot write" (*Theater*, vol. 9, no. 1 (1977), p. 51). And to Bernard Dort he revealed (*Travail théâtral*, 1972, p. 31):

There are some initial drafts that I worked on with Sturm: a general outline of the development of the show and several arrangements concerning the people who were to group around the barricade – a barricade in which each stone, each gun would have been genuine, and which would have been constructed in the course of the evening. That was the idea: for us the Commune represents the end of barricades, their swan-song. And the theme that we would have dealt with was the end of the bourgeois conception of revolution and the appearance of another form of revolution with entirely different aesthetics, with an entirely different mode of representation, with other metaphors of revolution since the Commune. I think that this is an interesting topic for the theatre.

In place of the Commune project, which, though "finally abandoned" on 14 December 1971 (Protocol no. 170), continued until 1975 at least to be reconsidered, Stein and his actors turned their attention again to the Russian Revolution. *The Mother* had spanned the period from 1905 to 1917. Now Stein's next production of an overtly political piece took up events in the immediate post-revolutionary period, during the Russian civil war. This was Vsevolod Vishnevsky's *Opti-*

mistic Tragedy (Optimistische Tragödie) which opened at the Schaubühne on 18 April 1972.

The play, written in 1932 and premièred the following year in
Kiev, was based on Vishnevsky's own experiences during the civil
war. It describes how a group of revolutionary anarchist sailors
docked in the Baltic are placed under the orders of a former Czarist
military Commander and a female Commissar. Despite initial resentment towards this discipline imposed from above and attempts to
resist orders from the newcomers, the sailors gradually submit to
authority. Marching for almost four thousand miles to fight against
the counter-revolutionaries on the southern front in the Ukraine,
they turn from anarchy to party discipline, and of the three anarchist
leaders one is killed, one deserts and the third finally lends his support to the Bolsheviks. United as the First Red Navy Regiment, they
at last engage the counter-revolutionaries and are all killed in battle.
Meanwhile the Second Red Navy Regiment is on its way to the
southern front. Hence the title: the piece is a "tragedy," since it
shows the deaths of the Red sailors; it is "optimistic," because others
will continue and win the revolutionary struggle.

The play is therefore primarily concerned with revolutionary
anarchism and revolutionary discipline. It was a theme of some relevance to the progressive thinkers of West Germany in 1972. Having
emerged from the heady days of student riots, sit-ins and public protest, there was now a need to consolidate the left and to work for
social change in a more sober manner. So, while the anarchist tendencies lived on, as in the violent acts of the Baader–Meinhof group,
more serious progress was sought in disciplined and restrained
political activity. This development was of particular relevance to the
experience of the Schaubühne actors, who themselves had passed
through a process of immediate and often almost anarchic self-deter-
mination, and were now seeking for revised structures in which
socially relevant theatre could function more efficiently.

This did not mean, however, that Stein imposed any topicality on
the piece. As he said of Optimistic Tragedy (Travail théâtral, 1972, p.
27):

The work seems to me to be much more topical if you don't introduce artificial references to current events, if you stick to the story as it is told, if you
give free rein to the imagination revealed in it – that is the way and the only
way that it can teach us something about anarchism today, about the difficulties inherent in every form of organization and about the objections that
can be raised in this area, and about the use to which the so-called democra-

cies of capitalism perennially put concepts of freedom . . . In *Optimistic Trag-edy* you can clearly see who was right but that doesn't prevent you from understanding the anarchists, from suffering with them. It is much more precise than current debates between reformism and revolution . . . To stress the point: when you are dealing with broad historical questions, you first have to clarify the distance which separates us from them.

It was therefore contemporary debate stimulated by historical example that once again attracted Stein to *Optimistic Tragedy*. At a meeting of the artistic staff on 6 September 1971 Sturm had already expressed his doubts about the Wekwerth–Palitzsch production of the piece at the Berliner Ensemble in 1958 (Protocol no. 132): "To define the ideological positions too rigidly is to kill the play stone dead, a typical mistake of the Berliner Ensemble. Its dynamic quality is what is positive about it. It creates images which are familiar to us through war films and Westerns."

The adaptation of the text, which was based on Friedrich Wolf's translation, thus emphasized the heroic struggle of the sailors. There were insertions of passages from contemporary accounts of the Red Army, and frequently Sturm and Steckel, the two *Dramaturgen*, went back to Vishnevsky's original version of the play – before it had been "corrected of its formalistic tendencies." Most importantly, it was decided to discard the final third of Vishnevsky's text, which deals with the continuing civil war, and to end the play with the death of the sailors. Even so, the Schaubühne version lasted three and a half hours.

In terms of casting, the production represented a striking example of the democratic spirit at the Schaubühne. Many "star" actors were relegated to small unnamed roles as sailors, Ganz, König and Rehm amongst them, and actresses like Clever, Lampe and Angela Winkler had walk-on parts without any lines at all. By contrast, Elke Petri, a relative newcomer to the Schaubühne, and incidentally like Michael König a member of the former German Communist Party (*KPD*), was given the leading role as Commissar.

This preparedness of the more talented actors to accept minor roles, a tradition which in Germany had its roots with the Meiningen troupe, has been admirable but has also created difficulties for Stein. The pressure to present plays of the type of *The Mother*, *Optimistic Tragedy* and *The Altercation*, did not stem solely from ideological con-viction, but because they gave the weaker members of the company parts of a reasonable size, and, in the case of the Workers' Theatre, offered opportunities to participate in directing. But, as Stein has said, it is not he that creates a hierarchy of roles but the plays themselves, and it is ultimately a waste of potential to give minor roles to the best actors. Just like Vishnevsky's anarchist sailors, the Schaubühne company had to find the balance between political idealism and the most effective use of resources.

As usual, the cast for *Optimistic Tragedy* underwent a period of careful preparation in the winter months of 1971–2. They watched twelve Soviet films dealing with the civil war and the Revolution (e.g. Eisenstein's *October 1917*) and also saw the television version of Wekwerth's production of *Optimistic Tragedy*. The actors themselves also prepared about ten papers on aspects of the civil war, on the history of Russian anarchism and so on. The reading-list, reproduced in the programme, comprised sixty-three titles!

Part of the preparation also consisted in looking at pictures and photographs of the period. At an early rehearsal the cast commented on the "posed, frozen and concentrated" quality in the attitudes of the Red soldiers fighting with bayonets. The actors then tried to reproduce this quality in the mimed battle which was to end the first half of the play. As Stein insisted: "The movements should be powerful not jerky, balletic rather, with great tension in the pauses between the different stages of movement" (rehearsal Protocol, 14 March 1972).

The "balletic" choreography of this battle sequence indicated the essentially non-realistic style of the production. The set, designed by Klaus Weiffenbach, consisted of a large inclined rectangle, on two sides of which the audience sat. For the first part of the play half of the stage opposite the audience was raised across the diagonal to represent the side of the sailors' ship. In the second part this half was lowered to provide an open area on which the discussions and battles could take place. As Stein explained to Bernard Dort (*Travail théâtral*, 1972, pp. 32–3):

the characters are not put on display in a privileged space. The space here is the bridge of the boat or the country where the fighting takes place; the spectator is placed on the same level as the bridge or the ground . . . the important thing is that in this way you can follow the broad lines of movement that unroll in front of you – but you can't achieve a global perception of theatre scenes enclosed within themselves.

A backdrop of grey clouds and a setting sun lent an artificial atmosphere to the second half, as though the production were quoting rather than attempting to realize the story. The ending too had something of the same quality. The sailors fought to the death, and from above red cloth was lowered to cover their bodies while a voice-over announced the departure from the Baltic of the Second Red Navy Regiment.

The acting too eschewed a strongly realistic style. Throughout the rehearsal period Stein urged his actors to play in a way that would have heroic dimensions and would present the major lines of the play without the distraction of trivial verisimilitude: "There should be more 'argumentation' than 'realistic mumbling' "; "The crowd scene has still to be freed of naturalistic imprecision and irrelevancies"; "Stein is opposed to solving contradictions by presenting psychologically motivated reactions. He would prefer to set broadly stated contrary attitudes [*plakativ-konträre Haltungen*] 'coldly' opposite one another, to amplify the areas of tension with historical commentary" (rehearsal Protocols for 14 and 15 March, 8 April). Similarly, as late as the preview, the sound of single shots was cut,

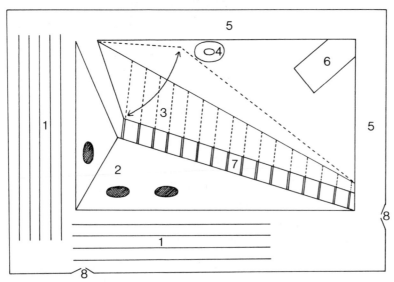

Fig. 6 Vishnevsky's *Optimistic Tragedy*. Groundplan, designed by Klaus Weiffenbach.

1 Audience seating (capacity 330). Rows to the left placed on the original stage area
2 Triangular sections sloping down towards the steps and containing large "portholes" for some entrances and exits
3 Raised portion representing ship's side and revealing broad steps
4 Ship's funnel
5 Catwalks sloping away to upper right corner
6 Removable portion for battle trench at end
7 Steps rising towards bottom right corner
8 Public entrances from foyer

because they were "on the one hand particularly enervating, on the other seemed thoroughly naturalistic."

Instead of giving the impression of naturalistic spontaneity, the production depended on the quality familiar from the confrontations and gun-battles of Westerns, which establish their own idiom and in which individual psychological realism distracts rather than deepens. It was appropriate therefore at moments of tension that atmospheric music, composed by Peter Fischer, should be played, and that the crowd scenes should appear unashamedly choreographed while never indulging in movement for its own sake. The anarchists were quickly defined as shabby, demoralized, bored and frustrated, easy prey to sex and liquor, ready to organize themselves in a primitively democratic but arbitrary manner. For example, an old woman

5 Vishnevsky's *Optimistic Tragedy*. The Commissar (Elke Petri) arrives amongst the anarchist sailors.

(Katharina Tüschen) accused one of the sailors of stealing her purse. He was summarily executed by being thrown overboard in a tarpaulin. Soon after she discovered her purse; so it was her turn to be drowned.

Into this rough world, where the will of the majority steered perilously close to mob rule, came the Commissar, a young, seemingly vulnerable, well-educated girl. She entered down the flight of steps at the end of the boat, a solitary figure, the tightly grouped sailors looking up towards her. One sailor detached himself from the group and moved up the steps towards her – an ambiguous move, half welcoming, half menacing. She approached with the kind of boldness that stems from nervousness and soon found herself the object of the sailor's lust. Music could be heard as one sailor reached deep into his trousers to pull up his shirt. He then paused and pulled it off sharply. The Commissar with simple and economical movements drew her pistol and shot him. For a moment she remained absolutely motionless ("like a photograph" – rehearsal Protocol, 7 March 1972).

The Commissar, played by Elke Petri with just the right measure of awkwardness and vulnerability, created her character from the demands of the situation. Any individual psychologizing would have been inappropriate here too, not only from aesthetic considerations, but also because – as with the proletarian figures of *The Mother* – it would have gone against the ideological implications of the piece. As Stein said to Dort (*Travail théâtral*, 1972, p. 28):

The Commissar personifies a mission . . . A character . . . like the Commissar can disappear, it will not destroy what she has achieved or has helped to establish. On the contrary. We can distance ourselves from the event and see that a whole epoch has now passed but that, thank God, what it has achieved remains and constitutes a historical fact against which we have to measure ourselves today.

By contrast, the chief anarchists were permitted a certain individuality, for – like the bourgeois figures of *The Mother* – they had not yet entered into the revolutionary collective. However, they restricted themselves to broad characterization without naturalistic details. Peter Fitz as their leader distinguished himself in appearance by a long leather greatcoat, and in manner by a weary and worldly wise sulkiness. Otto Sander as Hoarse-Voice used his hoarseness as his distinguishing feature; what in another production might have been crude characterization through the adoption of a single mannerism, was here an appropriate and economical way of setting Hoarse-Voice apart from his fellows.

Most impressive was Ulrich Wildgruber, an experienced and mannered actor, who subsequently worked a great deal with Zadek. Here, his appealing presence on stage, a charm which English audiences would find very congenial, and his habits of raising his voice at the end of sentences and of widening his eyes to give emphasis, gave just the right level of individuality to the coarse and likeable figure of Alexei, the only one of the leading anarchists finally to submit himself to discipline. As Peter Iden commented: "Never before have we seen this actor come so close to portraying the truth. Stein, who always discovers from his actors what he can teach them, helped him to control his lack of discipline, his vagueness and his diffuseness . . . We were able to observe an actor making a break-through into himself" (*Die Schaubühne*, p. 143).

The production which ran for twenty-seven performances was not considered a great success, although, as was by now common at the Schaubühne, it played to capacity audiences. As ever, Stein seemed to be caught in the crossfire from both right and left. Right-wing public and critics were alienated and bored by the revolutionary scenario; left-wing audiences tended to be suspicious of the polished, occasionally mannered, style of the production. As Stein said (*Travail théâtral*, 1972, p. 35):

If we'd performed *Optimistic Tragedy* in underpants or boiler-suits, if we'd shouted the lines, people would not have had fewer reservations about the political content of the piece . . . on the contrary. And I believe that such a conception of the theatre – a militant and, to some extent, puritanical theatre, lacking any attractiveness or variety – would today have no chance of affecting the sensibilities of the audience – an audience which is primarily bourgeois. And it wouldn't affect mine either. While working on *Optimistic Tragedy* I was fascinated by the writings of Babel and also by Lenin's telegrams . . . But Babel is much more beautiful. Economic reports can send me to sleep; but not Babel.

The reference to "beauty" in connection with political theatre seems strangely inappropriate, indeed for many theatre groups verging on anathema, but it was an identification sought after by Brecht and consistently pursued by Stein. As Bruno Ganz stated: "I really don't understand the objection that everything is too perfect. Somewhere and somehow Marxism must be realized. This embraces utopian elements, yearning after a structure that allows people to live and be together in freedom. You have to prepare the ground for this, and part of the preparation is the creation of beauty" (*Spielplatz*, 1 (1972), p. 57).

The beautiful, non-realistic, choreographed elements of the production tended in the direction of opera and film, and it seems that, already at this time, Stein had leanings towards more visual media. He certainly regards his direction of the videotape of *Optimistic Tragedy*, which he completed in fifteen days, as his best piece of work in television. The videotape record of his productions, which had begun with *Tasso* and now became a regular feature of Stein's work, fulfilled three functions. First, it preserved something after the curtain had fallen, the best possible documentation of this ephemeral art. Secondly, it provided an extra source of income for Schaubühne actors who are forbidden by contract to accept any work outside the ensemble. Thirdly, it gave Stein the opportunity of exploring a new medium which – despite frictions with the television technicians and directors – was to stretch him and ultimately lead him to make a full-length film.

But, for the time being, Stein's preoccupation was that the Schaubühne's emphasis on overtly political theatre was limiting its potential and was failing to discover a genuine confrontation with its largely middle-class audience. At a discussion about the forthcoming programme on 4 October 1971 (Protocol no. 136), he did not believe "that our audience should repeatedly have its revolutionary beard stroked. We need to seek another way. What is so provocative about *Optimistic Tragedy* is the presentation of certain necessities which are not accepted by us." The other way that Stein chose was to seek out no longer the necessities of revolutionary progress but to point out the contradictions in bourgeois consciousness. Never again directing a piece of revolutionary theatre, Stein turned his attention instead to the bourgeois antecedents of the revolution.

5   The myth of bourgeois individualism – Ibsen's *Peer Gynt*

The theatre [is] a contradictory undertaking, in which the yearning for a rational explanation of the world (and this of course includes the desire to change the world) subsists side by side with the yearning to remember – to remember things as they once were, to recall possibilities, human possibilities deep in the past.   (Stein, *Die Zeit*, 2 January 1976)

Stein's renewed concentration on "bourgeois" theatre proceeded from three major considerations. First, it seemed more honest than pretending to perform for the proletariat where no genuinely proletarian theatre audience existed: "we must remain aware that we are eminently bourgeois artists, that we first have to change ourselves, that we have to reckon with an audience that is eminently bourgeois" (*Christ und Welt*, 4 September 1970). Secondly, with the exception of some Brecht, revolutionary plays offered very little scope for the particular qualities of the Schaubühne ensemble: "Our time is extremely difficult, spongy, differentiated, not well suited to theater. To present the technics of administration employed by the social-democratic state, on the stage – everyone would fall asleep after five minutes! It can't be dramatized!" (*Performance* 4 (1972), p. 72).

Thirdly, and most importantly, Stein believed that the most effective area of political involvement for the theatre must be in the exploration of the reality known and understood by the ensemble, not in projecting some imagined revolutionary reality where a revolutionary situation did not exist. As he argued to actors and members of the artistic staff at a meeting of 30 November 1975 (Protocol no. 502):

There is no possibility in the theatre of communicating something about the ideology of the working classes, because it does not exist as a reality which one could explore by means of a process of theatrical remembering. In the theatre one can only project optimistic ciphers about working-class ideology. The theatre cannot be a means of realizing the ideology of the working classes. This realization can only be achieved in practical political struggle. The means are those of the word, of writing, of pictures etc. and not the interaction which takes place between two or three people in an enclosed space in front of a maximum of 1300 people . . . The theatre has the advantage over a book or a film that it retains a certain utopian potential that several people on a stage communicate directly and that one may witness

66

this and imagine that one is participating in it . . . If one performs *Antony and Cleopatra*, I don't find that – at least this is how I think at the moment – any less politically valuable than if comments about the Emergency Laws are more or less read out on stage.

In similar vein, and perhaps spiced with a certain polemical enthusiasm, Stein declared to a group of secondary-school children on a television discussion programme (quoted in *Der Abend*, 21 July 1977):

I have no desire to peddle ideas. If I wanted to communicate ideas and I had the ability to express myself clearly and rationally, I wouldn't get up on stage and start weeping or laughing, portraying love or death . . . I refuse to put bad plays which deal with the so-called problems of the working classes in our programme just to prove how leftish we are . . . I get really annoyed when I see how young people's understanding of art has gone to the Social Democratic dogs . . . For example the slogan: "everyone has to understand everything. The theatre consists of ideas which will enlighten people fully about their problems so that they can go home and improve their lives . . ."

What is highly desirable in the economic field has only a deadening effect in the artistic sphere; for artistic activity derives from precisely the difficulty of being unable to come to terms with practical living. I believe that in art other criteria are valid. In any case one has to accept that artists create stories which one cannot immediately understand.

Predictably, Stein's sceptical declarations about "political theatre" and the affirmation of his interest in the bourgeois tradition, particularly of the nineteenth century, seemed to many like a betrayal of the socialist aims of the Schaubühne. In fact Stein had never confused complexity with mystification; even in plays like *Vietnam-Discourse* he had never used the stage for propaganda, and he considered it important, as a political act, to rescue the masterpieces of bourgeois theatre "from an erroneous tradition of thought and concepts" (*Kürbiskern*, 2 (1973), p. 337). Nevertheless, it appeared to many that Stein had after 1972 abandoned his progressive political stance. The right-wing press were delighted; the left were dismayed, even suspecting that the fearless campaigner Stein was now intimidated by the risk of losing subsidies, and construing the commercial success of the Schaubühne as a reactionary symptom. A typical attack came from Peter Rühmkorf, an unsuccessful playwright, in an article in the first issue of the Rowohlt Verlag *Literaturmagazin* in 1973. Referring to "Peter Stein's delicatessen theatre," he demanded a "purposeful instruction" of the public. "We've put up long enough with the theatre as a subsidized cloud chamber. For us theatre as the undialectical mirroring of a world which has been shaped to make 'a scene' has had its day. And dialectics means for us: now we'll hit back" (p. 71). To which Stein would no doubt reply: tell me first who or what you intend to hit and then convince me that theatre is the best weapon to use.

Possibly more serious than these forays from without was the unease felt within the ensemble itself. I have already mentioned the decline in administrative participation, the failure of the specific group theatre, and resentment harboured particularly by frustrated technical staff. All of these early difficulties led inevitably to confrontations. The 1972–73 season saw not only the departure of Schwiedrzik but also that of the actress Elfriede Irrall who had taken over Therese Giehse's role in *The Mother*. In an explosive and detailed circular she explained her reasons for going. Apart from complaints about aspects of working conditions, she was alarmed by the direction in which the Schaubühne was heading: "The preoccupation with our bourgeois antecedents or with their cultural tradition is contemplative and is not designed to bring about change" (undated cyclostyled circular). To which Stein again would reply: in our social and historical situation the contemplation of our own traditions is the aspect of theatre in which we can most profitably engage and one which does bring about change – a change in the consciousness of the bourgeois audience.

Even before the founding of the new Schaubühne, Stein had, in February and March 1970, "contemplated" one aspect of the bourgeois tradition – in a short television piece made by Sender Freies Berlin based on a classic German nursery-rhyme collection, *Struwelpeter*. This piece, directed by Dietmar Buchman and Stephan van Ballaer at the German Film and Television Academy of West Berlin, showed Stein working with his actors, amongst them Otto Sander, on an interpretation of the story of Zappelphilipp, the boy who, unable to sit still at table, comes – like all the figures of *Struwelpeter* – to a disastrous end. Even here, in a children's nursery-rhyme, Stein adopted a critical stance to the ideology reflected in it. Referring to the savage morality of these rhymes, he explained to the actors: "This was the way the bourgeoisie ruined the lives of their offspring."

The same charm, combined with a suspect ideology, characterized the "adventure story" of Ibsen's *Peer Gynt*, which was Stein's first production of a bourgeois classic at the Schaubühne and the first time that he had directed a nineteenth-century play. It was originally intended that Claus Peymann should direct *Peer Gynt*, but by August 1970 he had decided against it. He later anyway had such difficulties with an ensemble that was ready repeatedly to challenge his methods and question his judgment that he left on 1 February 1971 after his one production at the Schaubühne, Handke's *Der Ritt über den Bodensee* (*The Ride Across Lake Constance*), premièred on 23 January 1971. Stein gratefully took up the task, since he had anyway declared himself "full of enthusiasm" for *Peer Gynt*. A play that excited him, the theatre structure that he had been seeking for years, the added pressure of the need to impress the Senate to release the blocked subsidies, and the collaboration of the *Dramaturg* and writer, Botho Strauss – all these things were spurs to Stein's creative impulse in his first major production at the Schaubühne. Spread over two evenings, *Peer Gynt* opened on 13 and 14 May 1971 and proved to be the most spectacular production by Stein until *Shakespeare's Memory* five years later and is still considered by many to be Stein's best piece of direction ever.

Discussion of the play had already taken place amongst the artistic staff of the Schaubühne over a year earlier, when it was recognized that Peer would provide an excellent model of *petit-bourgeois* adventurism with the inevitable outcome of the recognition of his own worthlessness: "By taking *Peer Gynt* we could attempt to develop an understanding of our own bourgeois origins. In the image of the onion [in Act v Peer peels off the layers of an onion but finds nothing at the centre], for example, a basic attitude of the bourgeoisie is revealed: search for identity, permanent self-castration, the longing to return to the womb" (Protocol, 5 April 1970, *Peer Gynt. Dokumentation der Schaubühnen-Inszenierung*, p. 67). At the first full production meeting (21 October 1970), Stein asked: "How can we approach *Peer Gynt*? In this play, more occurs to you, the better you know the nineteenth century. It's like your own grandfather: you partly recognize yourself in him and yet on the whole he seems a stranger" (*ibid.*, p. 68).

In order to get to know this familiar but strange ancestor better, all the cast, over six months before the production opened, began to prepare themselves for work on it. The nineteenth century was studied, as were the life and letters of Ibsen. Predictably, relevant writings of Marx and Engels were included, but, more surprisingly, there were also papers to be prepared on the adventure novels of Karl May and on Alfred Jarry. Stein and Strauss had at an early stage become aware that much of the character of the play was like that of the trivial novels of the nineteenth century and that the larger-than-life figure of Peer was in many respects closer to Jarry's Ubu than, for example, to Goethe's Faust. Although, as one of some fifteen papers, Strauss wrote on the philosophical influences on Ibsen, little attention was paid to the writings of Kierkegaard. Admittedly, Ibsen himself denied a direct influence from the Danish philosopher but Kierke-gaard's thinking nevertheless seems to permeate *Peer Gynt.* It was perhaps inevitable, though, that the "father of Existentialism" should not be allowed to distract the Schaubühne team from their primarily political and economic analysis of the play.

In pursuit of this, certain significant cuts and changes were made to the text. Ibsen's symbol of total commitment, the lad who chops off his finger to avoid conscription, was cut, partly because the scene consists almost entirely of narrative, but above all because it was felt by Stein and Strauss that this act of violent self-mutilation was no satisfactory alternative to Peer's spirit of compromise. As a result of this decision, the speech of the priest in Act v (at the graveside of the same man) had to be cut, and instead the funeral procession becomes that of Ingrid, the girl Peer had abducted in his youth. In place of the more mystical elements at the end, Strauss composed passages which related more closely to the political interpretation of the piece. Thus the Strange Passenger, instead of asking Peer about his experience of "dread," now posed questions like: "What do think of the controversy about the crisis of the individual? "Have you at any time in your life felt any concern about one or more of your fellow men?" "Have you ever tried to find out the facts about social conditions in Norway?" (*Peer Gynt Dokumentation*, pp. 144–5). The figure of the Thin Man, the devil/photographer, who meets Peer near the end, was also cut, thus lending even greater stature to the Buttonmoulder, who, as we shall see, was not played so much as Ibsen's retributive force but as a representative of the new technol-ogy. Despite these cuts, the production ran for six and a half hours, and it was decided at an early stage to perform it over two evenings, at the risk of a certain lack of continuity.

Because all the actors participated in developing a view of the play and were consulted about the structuring of the text, there was a clarity and consensus of understanding which assisted considerably in this colossal undertaking. As Bruno Ganz said (*Spielplatz*, 1 (1972), p. 55):

We didn't just go and abandon ourselves to the play. We were wary of crawl-ing inside the play and of suddenly saying: "We'll make a total denunciation of the *petite bourgeoisie* and we'll put all the trolls in evening-dress." It was decided well in advance how much of the fairy-tale element we wanted to retain and with it the whole naively evocative picture-book quality of the nineteenth century, so that we didn't suddenly get the idea of throwing away everything that was fabulous.

The casting, which was finalized on 2 March, had some interesting features. It had been decided to cut the figure of Helga, Solveig's young sister, as the ensemble did not wish to involve any children in the production, so – with plenty of doubling – all the parts could be filled from within the resources of the company. The democratic process of casting went smoothly enough, except that Stein objected to the decision by the ensemble to cast Rita Leska as the Woman in Green, since he foresaw difficulties in working with her on this role. However, he agreed to abide by the majority decision. At the initial casting discussions on 19 and 20 February, it was proposed that Peer should be played by at least three different actors. The reasons were threefold: first, the demands on the virtuosity of a single actor who must move from youth to old age in the course of the play; secondly, the dividing up of the role would be much fairer and in accordance with the ensemble ideal of the Schaubühne; thirdly, this decision would reinforce the critique of the individual and demonstrate how the central figure was conditioned by the circumstances of his life. Eventually it was agreed that the eight stages of Peer's life should be played by six different actors.

Initially it was thought that the different Peers would pass on some part of their costume – like the baton of a relay race – but this was not found to be necessary. Instead, the change was usually effected by adopting the physical position of the preceding Peer: so Peer no. 2 lifted Ingrid off Peer no. 1's shoulders and continued the abduction; when Peer no. 2 lay unconscious after ramming his head against a rock, Peer no. 3 lay down beside him, and the follow-spot which had been resting on the former Peer now swung across on to him to begin the next scene.

The titles of the different episodes were announced over loudspeakers, thus emphasizing the epic quality of the material. In the manner of a story-book the announcements helped to narrate the story, often in the past tense and referring to chapters rather than scenes. So the fifth act was preceded by the following (*Peer Gynt Dokumentation*, p. 143):

Peer left Egypt and journeyed back to America. He once more sought his fortune, as gold-digger and fur-trapper. But he had no success. Peer had grown twenty years older and longed to return home. The last chapter of the second part shows

Peer no. 8
The emblem of the onion.

As will be seen from this style, the announcements were not so much Brechtian devices of "alienation" as means of making reference to stories of adventure. This was particularly obvious in the way the two evenings were bridged. The first evening ended with phrases reminiscent of the extravagant promise of a Victorian theatre bill (*ibid.*, p. 137):

The second part is entitled "In Foreign Parts and the Voyage Home" and shows Peer's adventures in search of his fortune and his true self. You will see: fabulous riches, an exploding ship, monkeys and harem girls, statues of Memnon, a sphinx and a mirage, titillating love scenes, a mad-doctor and seven suicides, the return home with shipwreck and in terror of death, an eerie burial, schnapps and onions, a modern engineer and some figures familiar from the first part.

Everywhere danger threatens. Will Peer reach his goal? Will he find his own true self? Tomorrow evening at 8 o'clock: Peer Gynt, Part Two: "In Foreign Parts and the Voyage Home."

The second evening then began with a brief recapitulation of the first four episodes, with the first four Peers re-enacting moments from the first part, linked by narrative from the loudspeakers.

The story-book quality of the piece, which was also emphasized in the chosen subtitle of the production: "A play of the nineteenth century," clearly required a set on which the spectacular epic could unfold. As Stein insisted at the first production meeting on 21 October 1970 (*ibid.*, p. 69):

We shall require a very complicated set in terms of organizing the space and it will have to be ready before we begin. This will involve taking important decisions in advance. The arrangement of the set should allow Peer Gynt to make his grand journey through the whole theatre but also permit certain places, e.g. [Solveig's] hut, to be visible all the time. When the yacht sinks, for example, there will have to be bangs and splashes, etc.; otherwise it won't have sufficient clarity or comic effect. I think it's important to preserve a certain naivety in the presentation of the scenery. Such a production should incorporate fantastic effects of stage machinery and the contradictory quality that goes with it, namely that it never quite satisfies the demands made on it.

The design of the set was entrusted to Karl-Ernst Herrmann with whom Stein had worked in Munich on *In the Jungle of Cities* and who was now to become the leading resident designer of the Schaubühne. The whole length of the stage and auditorium area of the Schaubühne was used with the audience sitting on raised benches either side of the action. As Stein explained to Bernard Dort (*Travail théâtral*, 1972, p. 32): "For us it was important that the audience, sitting on the two galleries the whole length of the space, could be close to Peer's tribulations, near to the object which we intended to present." Immediately below the audience, therefore, was a large open undulating area, some 25 m by 10 m, where most of the action took place. Into the sand-coloured floor was set the sphinx, invisible until it was winched upright in Act IV. At one end of the traverse was a mountain, on which Peer built the hut for Solveig and himself and which opened up to reveal the troll kingdom. At the other end was a depression, which was used for the sinking of the yacht and

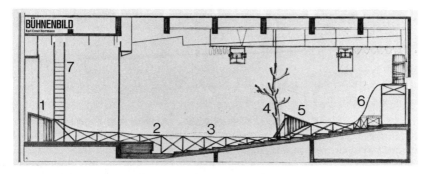

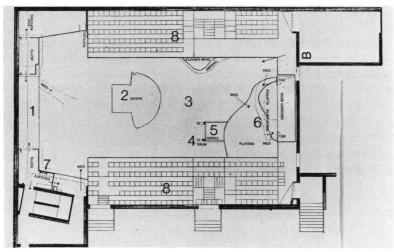

Figs. 7 and 8 *Peer Gynt*. Set design by Karl-Ernst Herrmann. Cross-section and groundplan.

1 Haegstad farm (I, iii) and seascape (IV, i–ii; V, i–ii) sited on the original stage area
2 Sphinx (erected for IV, xii–xiii)
3 Open area for Haegstad, Boyg, picnic, desert, harem and final scenes
4 Tree (IV, iv)
5 Mill (I, i)
6 Raised portion representing mountain, which opens to reveal trolls' cave
7 Ladder to work gallery
8 Audience seating (raked and on two levels)

Peer's shipwreck in Acts IV and V. One major advantage of this setting was that the audience could participate closely in the more intimate scenes at their feet while not being denied the grand spectacle
of the more fantastic moments of the plot. In addition, the large space
allowed simultaneous playing, so that, for example, throughout the
fourth and fifth acts (with the exception of the harem and madhouse
scenes) Solveig could remain visible in front of her hut, spinning
patiently while she waited for Peer's return.

The non-literal style of the story-book also affected decisions about
properties. When Bernard Dort suggested that Stein might be returning to a theatre of illusion like that of Max Reinhardt, Stein replied
(*Travail théâtral*, 1972, pp. 34–5):

> That's utter rubbish. *Peer Gynt* has nothing to do with that. Don't forget that
> the horses that appear are completely fake – they're stuffed horses. Reinhardt
> would have had real horses. They are only authentic in that they are genu-
> inely stuffed. Like the cat on the table [Aase's cat] – that's stuffed too. Every-
> thing that is used, or let's rather say quoted, creates an illusion to a certain
> extent but it does so almost in passing. Besides, all these objects and prop-
> erties have a part to play in *Peer Gynt*. They are like exhibits in a museum –
> the museum which exists in Peer's head and which Ibsen describes as such.
> We deliberately and polemically emphasized that all that Peer Gynt does or
> thinks, all that a *petit bourgeois* with a little imagination can say, do or think
> has already been said, done or thought a hundred times, a hundred thou-
> sand times . . . and we have to approach these things like pictures, objects
> and mummies which are displayed in museums. They are all second-hand
> things and objects with which it is impossible to do anything that is truly
> your own. To state this and to show it is an integral part of the performance.
> *Peer Gynt* describes an illusion. So I find it very funny when people accuse
> me of returning to a theatre of illusion.

Here we see once again how Stein's ideological and intellectual
understanding of a play coincides with his aesthetic decisions as a
director. In this realism–reality debate one is reminded of Peer
Gynt's story in Act V about the Devil and the pig. One day the Devil
decided to stage a performance, in which he claimed he would per-
fectly imitate the grunting of a pig. To assure himself of success, he
hid a pig under his cloak and pinched it to make it squeal. After-
wards the experts decided that the grunts and squeals were totally
unconvincing and that the whole presentation was grossly overdone.
In the same way, a real horse on stage is not a piece of reality but a
stylized object. Indeed, its very presence will render the performance
less real, because it does not share in the game that actors and audience are playing together. It may surprise; it will never convince.

So Stein used a stuffed horse on wheels, a stuffed cat, and a stuffed pig on wheels for Peer's entrance to the troll kingdom. The yacht that sank was a pantomime ship on a pantomime sea. All these objects were, as Stein said, "quoted," because what reality they achieved existed in the minds of the spectators not within the artificial confines of a theatre. By attempting to imitate reality, naturalistic theatre reveals its "real" world as an illusion: a live horse would have a reality quite distinct from this illusion and would shatter it. Instead of pretending to a reality impossible to achieve in the theatre, Stein prefers to show the cards up his sleeve, to let the audience see the wheels on his horse.

The ideological implications of this style were equally important. The theatre of illusion belongs to the bourgeois tradition of realism. Some Marxists, like the critic Georg Lukács, have argued that socialism should appropriate bourgeois realism for revolutionary ends. Others, notably Brecht, insisted that naturalism with its theatre of illusion could describe and celebrate reality but that it could not, within the limits of its form, criticize reality. As an aesthetic, naturalism in the theatre mystified the audience because it depended on the creation of an illusion; as a philosophy, by imitating reality, it ran the dangerous risk of acquiescing in existing circumstances.

In the Brechtian tradition, Stein did not wish to imitate reality but to criticize it, not to accept it as a *donnée* but to show it to be alterable. The stuffed horse, which communicates the idea of a horse without pretending to be one, is recognized as part of the phantasmagoria emanating from the mind of Peer Gynt. It is faintly ludicrous because, as a *petit bourgeois*, Peer cannot manage anything more individual or authentic than a taxidermist's product. Despite all his striving for individuality, Peer's head is full of consumer goods of the imagination.

The same critical distance was achieved in the acting. As Volker Canaris wrote of Peer no. 1 (*Theater heute*, 1971/13, p. 32):

When Giskes's Peer tells his mother Aase the story of riding on the stag, his eyes roll with excitement as he sees the sheer mountain ridges which he traces in the air with his fingers. When he shakes his mother with his fists, he seizes hold of the shaggy hair of the stag. When he swings his arms wildly, he rises with the monster off the ground, then plunges into the abyss, the pitch of voice falling with his own imagined descent. The means, which Giskes uses here, are neither narrative irony nor theatrical alienation – there is no distancing, no difference established between what is said and what is meant, between character and actor. Instead the character has at one and the same time the magic power of the story-teller who casts a spell over his listeners and the boastfulness of the charlatan that no one believes. Peter Stein has developed this style with his actors with staggering precision.

They act the role *and* criticize it. The bourgeois aesthetic of "embodying" a role has here been so perfected that it becomes a new style in itself, a critical dialectic, an aesthetic means to knowledge.

The character was realized but also quoted, made into an individual, but an individual representative of his time and of his class.

The critical distance from Peer no. 1 was also in part achieved by the remarkable performance of Edith Clever, for the first time playing an old woman, Peer's mother Aase. She managed to preserve a recognizable balance between scepticism about Peer's exploits and a deep-felt desire to be charmed by his lies, the same ambiguity of response invited of the audience. After depositing his mother on the roof of the mill, Peer went off to the wedding-feast at Haegstad (here, as throughout this chapter, I have used the spellings and names as given in *The Oxford Ibsen*).

The Haegstad scene creates difficulties for the director, because it is too artificially composed to sustain a realistic presentation, but without realism may easily become folksy and whimsical. Stein solved the problem by preserving the artificial quality of these storybook peasants while undercutting any jolly images of rustics in *Lederhosen* (rehearsal Protocol, March 1970, *Peer Gynt Dokumentation*, p. 120):

The wedding-feast is lifeless, the atmosphere is weary and mindless. The young men are already drunk, the girls dull and silly. Everyone is bored and waiting for something to happen. Things get exciting only when Peer arrives. He charges in from the troll mountain and tries to pounce on the girls straight away. They quickly set down their beer glasses and take to their heels, screaming and giggling. He pursues them with wild leaps and chases round after them on the open space in front of the two hills.

On Peer's first meeting with Solveig (Jutta Lampe), she made it quite clear that her broken garter was merely a pretext to escape from the infamous Peer, so that her deliberate return suggested an interest in Peer. This pious girl had a hint of knowingness in her manner. She was not to be a "figure off a kitsch postcard": "Solveig should not be stupid in the Haegstad scene; we should see that she understands very well what Peer wants from her and reprimands and rejects him from inner conviction." (18 and 19 February 1971, *Peer Gynt Dokumentation*, p. 71). This inner conviction, deriving from her Pietist upbringing, stood as an alternative to Peer's opportunism, but while Ibsen viewed this mystical path as positive (Solveig = Sun Way), Stein and his ensemble could not do otherwise than view Pietism as reactionary despite its communistic tendencies with regard to the sharing of property.

Peer's opportunism now led him into the abduction of the bride Ingrid (Sabine Andreas). Here again the economic aspects of this episode were emphasized: Ingrid as a prize rather than a sexual object. Stein and Strauss pointed out "that the crime against Ingrid is abduction not seduction . . . The Haegstad farmer must be furious with Peer because Ingrid is no longer a good match after the abduction" (18 and 19 February 1971, *ibid.*, pp. 71–2). Significantly, Peer's explanation in the original: "I was hot for a girl" was rendered in this version: "I was drunk," and Ingrid was costumed opulently to make her marketable value more obvious.

The economic aspects of sexuality were pursued in the scene where Peer encountered the three Herdgirls (Elfriede Irrall, Elke Petri, Angela Winkler). They were "a-socialized" because they no longer had husbands. When Peer came across them, they were all

6 Ibsen's *Peer Gynt.* Peer no. 1 (Heinrich Giskes) entertains the Haegstad peasants.

7   Moidele Bickel's design for the two-headed troll doctor's costume.

masturbating – a symbol of economic as well as sexual deprivation – and for them, within the bourgeois structure of society, Peer represented a "good catch." However, in contrast with Ibsen's version where Peer dances off with the Herdgirls, here they found him sexually (and economically) impotent and left him in disgust.

After his monologue (Act II, scene iv), which Michael König delivered as though suffering from a hangover after his carousing with the Herdgirls, he ran against an imaginary rock, producing a comic sound effect of flexitone, slide on the violin and jangled harp. Replaced by Bruno Ganz, Peer now lay sleeping, as the Woman in Green (Rita Leska) entered daintily on all fours. From a green satin dress emerged a hairy rump with a tail which she wiggled to the bird-song emanating from the loudspeakers. She crawled over Peer, sniffing around in his flies with her snout. He awoke to find himself facing her rear and leapt away in alarm, then crawled after her to kiss her backside blissfully.

Mounted on a pig, pushed by four singing and masked trolls, Peer and the Woman in Green approached the troll kingdom in the mountain. Again, the trolls are problematic figures in production. If they are too weird, Ibsen's point that they represent the *petite bourgeoisie* of Norway gets entirely lost; if they become too human, then the fairy-tale quality is lacking. Dieter Sturm warned against such a simple-minded satirical treatment of the trolls (5 April 1970, *Peer Gynt Dokumentation*, p. 68):

> We first have to show by theatrical means the power that the troll world has over Peer before we can attempt a critique of the trolls. If you start off by making them ridiculous in the crude manner of a satirical revue, you lose the critical attitude of the play. The line described by the play must be realized on stage. If you denounce everything point by point at the very moment that it arises, nothing will be achieved. That way you don't represent anything; that way you get the well-known effect of bourgeois satirical revues – the audience sit there howling with laughter without recognizing that it is they who are being represented on stage.

Sturm proposed therefore that the trolls needed to develop their own identity as trolls while making an obvious reference to the *petite bourgeoisie* they represented: "the trolls are colourful and kitschy, they are not portraits of the Norwegian *petite bourgeoisie* but their kitsch configurations, their garden dwarfs" (*ibid.*, p. 68). The trolls' costumes were generally shabby, ill-fitting versions of Victorian dress: wide, full-length dresses, tails, waistcoats; for one a top-hat and a cane, for the Troll King white trousers and boots. Of the costumes, designed by Moidele Bickel, Susanne Raschig and Joachim

Herzog, it was justly observed that they did not merely "clothe the actors but stimulated them to perform" (Hellmuth Karasek, *Die Zeit*, 21 May 1971). To render the trolls nightmare figures of Peer's imagination, they were given tails and grotesque masks, most pig-like with broad snouts, one with a colossal bulbous nose, the men balding or at most with sparse, etiolated white hair. The troll scene was regarded as a high-point of the production, a prime example of what *Theater heute* (1971/13, p. 19) described as a combination of "storybook naivety and analytical clarity."

The troll palace was set in the side of the mountain and contained the bourgeois accessories of upright piano and silver chiffonier with ornaments. The action of the scene is described in the rehearsal Protocols of 16 and 17 March 1970 (*Peer Gynt Dokumentation*, p. 119):

The grotesque troll figures with their animal masks could have the effect of a distorted nightmarish mirroring of the society of Haegstad. When the gates

8   Peer no. 3 (Bruno Ganz) in the troll palace.

of the troll mountain are thrown open, rags and cloths are spread out like fine carpets, and the sow with Peer and the Woman in Green riding on it is shoved and pulled into the hall of the Troll King [Otto Sander] by several young trolls.

When the sow reaches its central position, the Woman in Green is helped down by her sister who comforts her for being seduced by Peer, a human. Peer is surrounded by the trolls quietly and threateningly chanting the word "Slaughter," then they finally pull him down from the sow. He slides off and lands on the upturned soles of the young trolls who are lying on their backs with their knees drawn up to their chests. They hold him up for a while, spin him slowly round and finally drop him. Meanwhile the Troll King, supported by the troll courtiers and elders, has climbed on the sow's back, where he stands with legs apart watching the antics of his young subjects. Then he calls sharply and authoritatively for order: "Cool down!" . . .

The movement of the whole scene should be sluggish and should have the unreal quality of a dream. It is especially important that the masks – this "dead" material – should come alive: the trolls must put their hands to their mask-faces as if to a natural face.

After the gates to the troll kingdom banged shut, all went dark. Then in the darkness was heard the sound of Peer flailing about with a branch. This was his encounter with the Boyg, whose voice was that of Peer himself, still recognizable though electronically treated, and recorded in the aural vacuum of an acoustically "dead" room.

To end the first evening the stocky Wolf Redl replaced the slender, sensitive Bruno Ganz as Peer. To him fell the sections in which Peer erected a rickety hut for Solveig and himself, was turned aside from his happiness by the visit from the now aging Woman in Green with her ugly brat dressed in a sailor suit (Christof Nel), and finally went to his mother's bedside to comfort her with a dream journey as she died.

The second evening began with Dieter Laser playing the now rich and successful Peer. At one end of the theatre was the sea, represented by a blue cloth surmounted by regular white "waves." Floating at anchor was Peer's yacht, a large detailed cut-out model. At the other end of the stage Solveig's hut still stood on the mountain with the waiting Solveig before it. In the centre, beneath a white canopy, sat Peer picnicking with his three capitalist friends (Rüdiger Hacker, Günter Lampe, Rüdiger Kirschstein) – the Swedish businessman, Herr Trumpeterstraale, was cut in this version. Here, as ever, Stein revealed his acute eye for telling detail: when Peer admitted that his riches were due to trading in idols and slaves, the French and German capitalists leapt up in moral indignation; the Englishman remained seated. After the comic moment of the yacht's explosion, Peer was pursued by a lion – once again stuffed, its growl produced from the speakers, but "never successfully," as Peter Fischer ruefully admitted (*Peer Gynt Dokumentation*, p. 64). Climbing a tree, Peer was teased by two monkeys, played with great virtuosity by Hans Joachim Diehl and Tilo Prückner. Finding the Emperor's horse, Peer, once more played by Wolf Redl, rode into the harem where he was entertained by Anitra (Angela Winkler) and her four belly-dancing maidens.

For the penultimate section, "On the Track of the Past," Werner Rehm played Peer. The massive sphinx was raised from the stage, and this too became the setting for the scene in the lunatic asylum. Here Stein abandoned the restraint of his "quoting" style and played the scene with all the violence, horror and physical commitment of the Artaudian Theatre of Cruelty. Dusty and streaked with blood, most of them naked, the madmen crawled into the pit at the base of the sphinx, called forth by their director, Dr Begriffenfeldt (Hans

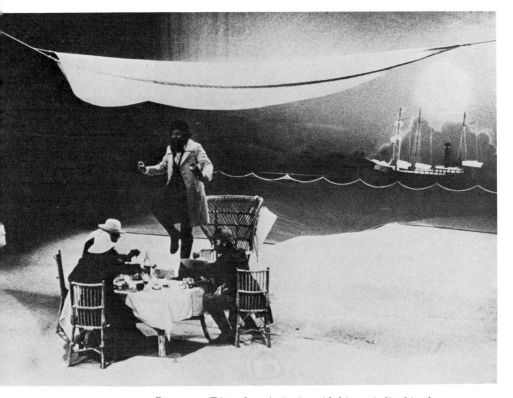

9   Peer no. 5 (Dieter Laser) picnics with his capitalist friends.

10   Peer no. 7 (Werner Rehm) in Begriffenfeldt's asylum under the
sphinx.

Joachim Diehl) (rehearsal Protocol, 9 April 1971, *Peer Gynt Dokumentation*, p. 124):

Begriffenfeldt's patients creep out of their cells, each one preoccupied only
with himself, each constantly pursuing his own tic. The first madman [Claus
Gärtner] sits numbly against the wall, staring at the palm of his hand and
playing with his penis. The second [Klaus-Harald Kuhlmann] lies on the floor
with his legs pulled up to him and his head hidden under his arms. The
third [Günter Lampe] lies on his back or on his side with one leg held firmly
against his body. The fourth [Christof Nel] kneels by the wall and urinates
incessantly. The fifth [Tilo Prückner] crouches on hands and knees, hangs
his head and turns round his own axis from time to time . . . From the cell
comes a poor Fellah [Willem Menne], his body doubled under the weight of
a mummy strapped to his back, who imagines he is King Apis. Begriffenfeldt, familiar with his patient's trauma, strokes the mummy. The Fellah

83

leaps before the startled Peer like an Egyptian relief (legs at full stride, torso turned to the front, angular arms). He bellows the name "Apis" in a high-pitched, almost cracking voice. He relaxes from this pose with an obviously painful and tense movement of the head. When Peer fails to answer his question satisfactorily he crumples, is racked with pain and wants to go back into his cell. Begriffenfeldt prevents him however and orders him to tell his tale of woe. Peer regards this story as the ravings of a lunatic, and when the Fellah asks him in desperation how he can prove that he is King Apis, Peer at first replies facetiously that he should build pyramids as magnificent as those of the person he identifies with. But this advice is of no use to the poor peasant and he asks for a better suggestion. Peer proposes that he might hang himself so that he would end up in the same state as the Apis mummy on his back. Peer sniggers behind his hand at his crazy idea and is then horrified to see that the Fellah actually sets about following his advice.

A similar horror was repeated when Hussein (Rüdiger Hacker), imagining himself to be a pen, sharpened his nib by cutting his throat. Finally all the lunatics committed suicide and Peer, now in a dead faint, was crowned Emperor of the Madmen by Begriffenfeldt with a crown made of straw.

Even here, amidst this Artaudian violence, the political dimension was maintained: lunacy, the exclusive obsession with oneself, is but the most extreme form of capitalist selfishness. So as Peer's consciousness slipped away, he cried – not as in Ibsen, "I'm whatever you want – a Turk, a sinner, a troll" – but here, "I'm whatever you want – a liar, a capitalist, a troll."

In the fifth act Bruno Ganz played the aging Peer. The ship was created by a swaying circular area with mast, ropes and railings, suspended in a single spotlight over the "sea." After the shipwreck Peer and the Cook were seen struggling above the waves – the sea cloth raised to a height of one and a half metres – like two figures in a grotesque puppet theatre. The Strange Passenger came riding up astride a barrel to put his searching questions to Peer.

Once on land, Peer encountered the funeral procession, at the end of which the coffin fell open to reveal the body of Ingrid. The goods auctioned in the original text were now replaced by a pile of Peer's belongings littering the roadside. Having failed to be recognized by the now dirty and impoverished companions of his youth, Peer searched for food by gathering wild onions. Peeling an onion, Peer failed to find any centre, just as his own life, after peeling off all the layers of his adventures, had no centre to it. So he was ready to meet the Buttonmoulder (Claus Gärtner), a mystical figure in the original whose function is to melt down the souls of the worthless.

Here, in the most radical interpretative shift of the Schaubühne version, the Buttonmoulder in black coat and tall top-hat introduced himself as "Engineer Buttonmoulder." Appearing with his workers, he explained to Peer in the technological officialese of the new age (*Peer Gynt Dokumentation*, p. 146):

The firm that we represent is starting a far-reaching campaign of clearance and development in the Gudbrandsdal . . . We shall have to take especial care that insignificant individuals, unworldly poets and persons of independent means, as well as the entire retrogressive middle classes do not stand in the way of progress, but on the contrary accelerate it. These species shall – if I may put it this way – be the lubricating oil that keeps the wheels of our economy running smoothly. To put it in concrete terms: you and your sort will go into the melting pot to be converted into new raw material.

What in Ibsen was the ancient mystical insight that only by annihilating the self can selfhood be achieved ("To be one's self is to kill one's self"), became in the Schaubühne version the Marxist argument that only by releasing hold of the bourgeois concept of individuality and entering into the collective could one fulfil oneself and create the social circumstances where self-fulfilment became a possibility for all and not merely for a privileged few. The ending, which was originally to have involved the complete dismantling of the set, was designed to show the bankruptcy of the concept of individuality in an age of technical reproduction (*ibid.*, p. 73):

The main problem about developing a conception for the last part of the play is to show the reason why we have performed this extensive spectacle, a reason that must emerge from the action itself. The ending provided by Ibsen, the morality play which is appended, and above all the sentimental closing image of Solveig and Peer are passages where we cannot remain faithful to the text. But the production should not treat this ending ironically or destroy it but use and adapt it meaningfully.

After encountering the Buttonmoulder/Engineer and failing to convince him – or the Troll King who reappeared – of his need to be preserved as an individual, he finally returned to Solveig. In Ibsen, Peer is redeemed by Solveig's faith, hope and love; here the intended ending was somewhat different:

Peer goes to Solveig, who, now blind and aging, is still waiting for him, and he asks her to confirm that he was himself. She does this by declaring that in her love, in her hope and in her faith he has always been himself. Peer imagines that he is redeemed, and lowers himself onto Solveig's lap with relief and curls up on it. Meanwhile the workers [the Buttonmoulder's assistants] have quietly gathered together at the foot of the mountain on which Solveig's hut stands and watch the ending with emotion. There is a moment's silence, interrupted by the loud noise of machinery. The worker-actors begin to dismantle the hut with the Solveig–Peer "Pietà" tableau before it. During this machines appear, real machines which can produce something, e.g. Peer Gynt souvenirs, printed material, etc., and which are industriously attended by other worker-actors. The finished product – serial reproductions of Peer Gynt kitsch – will be transported on long conveyor belts and, sealed in transparent packages, will be distributed amongst the audience. The play *Peer Gynt* reduced to a souvenir. The whole thing would then be a living allegory of the anachronistic relationship of Peer's individualism myth to the actual state of development of industrial production even in his day, and at the same time a metaphor for the kitsch industry, which has always flourished before and since, and which propagates, in millionfold reproduction, myths about the individual genius in the form of novels, painting, etc.

In the event, pressure of time and the technical complexities of these proposals, meant that the machinery could not be introduced into the ending. Instead, the workers cleared the stage of its débris, sprayed the ground with disinfectant, began surveying and measuring the landscape, and drove the by now drunken mourners of Haegstad into the hollow where they were to be melted down. Peer crept into his foetal position on Solveig's lap, and the workers carried them both down from the mountain to the central area. Here a photographer took their picture as a more simple means of expressing the elaborate idea of manufacturing Peer Gynt kitsch souvenirs – the photograph as the endlessly reproducible image of the "individual."

As Günther Rühle commented on this final "Pietà" image (*Frankfurter Allgemeine Zeitung*, 26 April 1978):

the cold use of this melancholy pose made us recognize how worn out such stylization was, and the sad lamenting eyes of Jutta Lampe (Solveig) spoke of the terrible and unjust sacrifice of woman that her love concealed. The lie of this image of humility became apparent. With this cold image Stein distanced himself from the play. He seemed to be saying: "I have shown you what was once beautiful but must no longer be regarded as such" . . . In Jutta Lampe's dead eyes the drama suddenly seemed like a ghost, although because of its new-found freshness it had until then all seemed such fun.

With this ending Stein hoped to demonstrate the ultimate bankruptcy of the *petit bourgeois* individualism he had been at such pains to portray for over six hours. It was a good and responsible decision to allow the enchantment of Peer's story-book progress to work on the audience. As Sturm had said a year before the production: "If you denounce everything point by point at the very moment that it arises, nothing will be achieved." The danger, however, was that the enchantment would live on in the imagination of the audience and the critical sting-in-the-tail would be forgotten. Even if the Marxist analysis of the text made its impact, it remained an analysis and did not point towards any constructive alternative (the

11 *Peer Gynt.* The final "Pietà" image. Peer no. 8 (Bruno Ganz) crawls into the lap of the blind Solveig (Jutta Lampe).

Buttonmoulder/Engineer was closer to the commandant of a labour camp than to the apostle of a new age). As Michael König argued (Gerd Jäger *et al., Theater heute*, 1973/13, p. 44):

Peer Gynt did not show any way in which the *petite bourgeoisie* might be won for the revolutionary cause. We did manage to expose as pie-in-the-sky the dream of the *petit bourgeois* to live as a member of the *haute bourgeoisie*, we did show the hopelessness of Peer's efforts at "self" realization, but we did not show any revolutionary perspective.

Clearly, *Peer Gynt* did not make the same clear political statement as *The Mother* or *Optimistic Tragedy*. Equally clearly, it represented a searching and intelligent investigation into the alienation well understood by the sort of people who came to see the play. For Stein it was the first time that he was able to pull out the throttle of the superb machine he had helped to create. All the resources of the Schaubühne were devoted to this undertaking, and Stein threw himself into work with almost obsessive energy: "I did everything from directing the play to cleaning the toilets" (unpublished Bergmann interview, 1978). He expected from his actors and technicians the same total commitment. Despite vehement protests he insisted that the four harem girls should push the large horse bearing Peer and Anitra; he stubbornly refused requests to use something other than cement for the dust in the madhouse scene. ("First I'm all in favour of obstinacy, secondly I'm not very imaginative" – Stein, Protocol no. 107, 26 May.) Above all, he became so preoccupied with the play that his normal friendly relationship with the actors seemed under threat. Certainly, there was good reason why Stein became tense. The set, properties and masks, all of which were to have been ready at the earliest stages of rehearsal, took much longer in the making than had been predicted. The first formal rehearsal took place on 22 February. The troll mountain was still being constructed on the rehearsal stage on 29 March. By 10 April the actors were begging Stein to postpone the advertised opening on 27 April. He called them "short-sighted and like fluttering sparrows," but later (26 May) apologized for this "explosion." On 1 May the first rehearsal could at last take place on the theatre stage, but the following day it was found that the troll mountain was too steep to push the pig up it. Even after the first night on 13 May, the following afternoon was devoted to a technical rehearsal for the second part. Then, on 17 May, further rehearsals had to be called to prepare Katharina Tüschen in the role of Aase, as Edith Clever was to become a mother in July.

Many of the tensions that developed between Stein and the technicians date from this time. Working himself from fourteen to sixteen hours a day, he was repeatedly irritated by union regulations allowing only eight hours before overtime. In the end, he and the actors all helped with the building of the set, and even then there was not time to present the ending as it had been intended; instead, it was "improvised and actually quite irresponsible" (Stein, Protocol no. 105, 21 May). It was pointed out, in fairness to the technicians, that the actor who commits himself totally is involved in a learning process and will develop as a result of the experience; but that "a carpenter who works on three night-shifts in a row will still be the same carpenter" (Protocol no. 106, 22 May 1971).

Undoubtedly, the rehearsal process was not a smooth one nor organized as efficiently as it might have been. The last scene was not rehearsed until 19 April, six weeks after the first scene had been rehearsed. The first complete run-throughs took place on the two days before the play opened. One actor complained that his own scene had been rehearsed for only two twenty-five minute periods before the run-throughs and that it was changed for the opening night. Other actors would work on their own in parallel rehearsals and found then that Stein had almost nothing to say in response to their work. This desire by actors for reassurance and approval is a perennial problem faced by most directors. As Stein said (Protocol no. 107, 26 May 1971): "If I think something's bad, I'll say so, but not if it's reasonably O.K. . . . There are certain difficulties in analysing and saying why I think something is good, because then nothing of it may remain at the next rehearsal."

Although the experience of directing *Peer Gynt* had not been completely positive, it taught Stein a great deal about the possibilities and limitations of working in a collective. It also resulted in a production of outstanding merit, which assured the Schaubühne of continued subsidies. Most importantly, for Stein as a director, it showed that his clarity, precision and intelligence could be applied not only to the close-up work of a play like *Tasso* but also to the vast spectacle of *Peer Gynt*.

6   From bourgeois past to bourgeois
     present – Kleist's *Prinz von Homburg,*
     Labiche's *Piggy Bank,* the *Antiquity
     Project,* Gorky's *Summerfolk,* Handke
     and Botho Strauss

Stein's next exploration of the bourgeois past took him back to a play
closer in style to *Tasso.* This was Heinrich von Kleist's *Prinz Friedrich
von Homburg,* which opened on 4 November 1972. Yet, curiously
enough, its theme based on a clash between discipline and anarchy
was not dissimilar from Stein's earlier production of that year, *Optimistic Tragedy.*

Prinz von Homburg was the last play Kleist wrote before he took his
own life in 1811. It was written against the background of Napoleon's
domination of Germany and was intended as a thoughtful but nevertheless reactionary contribution to Prussian nationalism. Based on
the Battle of Fehrbellin in 1675, when an army of 7,000 from Brandenburg (later to become Prussia) defeated 11,000 better equipped Swedish invaders, the play tells how Prince von Homburg disobeys orders
and launches his attack too early. Although his impetuous action
wins the day, he is condemned to death for his insubordination. At
first he cannot believe that his ruler, the Elector of Brandenburg, is
serious. Soon, however, he becomes terrified at the thought of death
and pleads for his life. The Elector will reprieve him if Homburg
agrees that his treatment is unjust. Since his honour will not permit
him this way out, Homburg accepts the sentence passed on him, and
goes serenely to his execution. At the last minute the Elector, having
won Homburg's loyalty, now frees him, and Homburg is hailed as
the victor of Fehrbellin.

Once again in this play Stein returned to his preoccupation with
the individual's relationship with the collective: here Homburg has
to subordinate his own individuality and impetuousness to the
authority of the Prussian state. Clearly, this state represents a false
collective: it is a military machine, it deals in moral absolutes (diso-
bedience is wrong even when it achieves victory), and its decisions
emanate not from the collective but from the will of its leader. It was,
therefore, an apparently curious choice of play for Stein. However, it

was characteristic of the work of the Schaubühne to rescue major writers of this kind (Kleist, Hofmannsthal, Hölderlin) from misappropriation at the hands of the Fascists. *Prinz von Homburg* was one of the most frequently performed classics of the Nazi stage, celebrating the conversion of a man beset by weaknesses into a strong and obedient hero and ending with the shout: "Into the dust with all the enemies of Brandenburg!"

For as long as Stein had worked in the theatre he had come into conflict with authority, either that of reactionary *Intendanten* like Everding or of municipal politicians in Zurich and Berlin. Beyond his own experience, the West German state seemed now in 1972 to be lurching towards the right after the tremors of the late sixties: there were the new Emergency Laws and the almost hysterical pursuit of left-wing anarchists. It perhaps seemed high time that he should examine the roots of the *Deutsche Misere* ("German misery"), the repeated tendency of one of the most energetic, talented and sensitive peoples of the world to subject themselves to obtuse and brutal authority.

It was a bold choice of play and one that was almost certain to confirm the worst fears of Stein's left-wing critics. Stein himself admitted his difficulties with the material. At the first discussion of the play on 26 May 1972 he confessed that he was still not clear what the theme of the play was, and said that while the Prince seemed "to talk a whole load of crap, he seemed tortured and rotting from within." Nevertheless, as Stein had already argued on 22 October 1970 (Protocol no. 32), *Prinz von Homburg* was "eminently suitable" to portray the *Deutsche Misere*; for, as he put it to Jack Zipes (*Performance*, 4 (1972), 75):

the German bourgeoisie in its weakness and irresoluteness had to experience how all its contributions, for example to the development of a national state or a national feeling, led to nothing more than a restorative strengthening of the Prussian feudal state to a major imperialist power. That's what's called the "German misery" and this play is a very essential contribution to understanding it.

In order to achieve the necessary critical distance from the piece, Stein and his *Dramaturg*, Botho Strauss, decided to go a step further than they had taken in *Peer Gynt*. In the Ibsen production they had set a great deal "in quotation marks" – spectacular episodes, elements of acting and so on. Now in *Homburg* they "quoted" the whole piece. The alternative title of the play was given as "Kleist's Dream of Prince Homburg." It opened with a voice-over announcing the title and author and reading Kleist's dedication of the piece to Prin-

cess Marianne of Prussia; it ended with an extract from Kleist's suicide note. In this way it was suggested that Homburg was not a historical figure of the seventeenth century but a dream creation of
Kleist in the early years of the nineteenth century: an embodiment of
Kleist's own Romantic yearnings for recognition and acceptance by
those in authority (and here, of course, the artist's desire to overcome
his alienation by integrating himself into the state is again close to
Goethe's *Tasso*). To this end Stein also made the production more
intimate than most performances had done, which often treated the
play as a pretext for a historical pageant: he reduced the fifteen characters and unspecified extras of Kleist's play to eleven characters,
played by ten actors. He also insisted on a simple set that would
emphasize the internal dream-landscape of the conception. Karl-
Ernst Herrmann, the designer, surrounded the stage and auditorium
with black velvet drapes and covered the floor in dark blue felt. For
the battle and execution scenes the drapes at the rear were raised to
a height of some two metres, revealing a back-drop with pale blue
sky and low hills stretching into the distance – a broad, brightly lit
horizon, a Utopia beyond the dark world of the Elector's palace. For
the burial of Froben a large block was pushed in from behind so that
the black velvet fell over it to form a catafalque. Three large candle-
sticks were placed either side of it, and with extreme simplicity the
oppressive ritual of a military funeral was achieved. As in *Tasso,* the
open area of the set allowed for simultaneous action: while Homburg
was imprisoned in his room, his grave (in a trap with real earth) was
being dug; the Elector sat visible, while Homburg struggled with his
own terror of death. Stein hoped, however, in terms of visual presentation to go beyond *Tasso,* where he felt that they had not "escaped
from the ghetto of coming to terms with the language" (Protocol no.
221, 21 June 1972). The strongest visual moment was the ending,
where Stein found an even more theatrical means than in *Tasso* to
ironize the conclusion. In the earlier production Bruno Ganz was carried off on the shoulders of Werner Rehm (Antonio), a monkey
tamed by the court; here Ganz as Homburg lay in a faint on the
ground, as the jubilant officers raised a life-size dummy of Homburg
onto their shoulders to bear off the figure who had become a "puppet" of the Prussian state.

The costumes, designed by Moidele Bickel, also avoided historical
accuracy in order to reinforce the timeless quality of the dream. Stein
wanted a "noble simplicity" in the costumes and wanted above all to
avoid the effect of a fancy-dress ball (discussion after first read-
through on 2 September 1972). At the first run-through on 22 October

12 Kleist's *Prinz von Homburg*. The final image. Homburg is carried off as a puppet.

1972 he was still insisting on changes, since the costumes "did not so much give the impression of an idealized army as the autonomous effect of a cabinet of curiosities." Finally, however, the loosely fitting trousers buttoned the whole length of the side-seams, the wide-sleeved white shirts with crossed leather straps or light breast-plates, and the full-length cloaks for the final scene achieved the quality defined in the programme note on costumes: "The military personnel of *Prinz von Homburg* does not really belong to any period – these cavalry generals and colonels of Kleist are all idealized officers, they are figures in the author's vision of a poeticized, humane, military community. That is why they wear light and beautiful fantasy uniforms."

Although the piece had a fluid dream-like development (despite changes of time and place the scenes up to Homburg's arrest were played without a break), the epic elements of Stein's style were still

93

in evidence. The presence of the Elector on stage during Homburg's scenes in his room contained the narrative implication: "Meanwhile the Elector sat in his room weighing up the situation." When Golz (Peter Fitz) delivered his report of the battle, he did not as in Kleist address the Electress and Princess, but "turned to the audience, with cool analysis. In this way he draws the complete attention of the audience towards the narration and they are not distracted by watching an actor perform" (rehearsal Protocol, 18 September 1972).

The major thrust of the acting, however, was to establish the idealized, dream-like quality of the piece so that the Prussian military ethos could be unmasked as a dangerous illusion. Not only was Homburg to be portrayed as somnambulistic, but the world he inhabited became a dream-world of sleepwalkers heading for the abyss. Even Kleist was uncertain of the substantiality of the world into which Homburg "awakes": "Is it a dream?" asks Homburg after surviving his "execution." "A dream – what else?" replies Gollwitz.

Stein spent several rehearsals working with Ganz on Homburg's somnambulism, a good example of the detailed physical involvement that Stein expects of his actors. At the first rehearsal on 3 September 1972 Stein offered the following suggestions to Ganz: his walk should be "aimless, indefinite"; he easily loses direction; movement should come from tilting the body forwards; it is important where the eyes focus – either on the horizon or immediately in front of him – but he never actually sees anything; he should include searching movements; he should listen to sounds we cannot hear; he must not look feeble; the silent introductory sequence should last five to ten minutes but one must avoid making the mistake of prolonging it too much – otherwise it would become like the concentration exercise of the actor in the Living Theatre's *Mysteries* which only led to ridicule or admiration for the actor's stamina; the searching must not become hectic; somnambulism is a state of bliss; there should be no inhibitions, no fear, no safeguards; it is not the eyes but the whole face which sees; one might perhaps carry out dangerous movements, crossing a plank, moving over a mound and so on. On 13 September Stein and Ganz returned to working on the opening sequence and now concentrated on the physical actions involved. Suggestions now included: keeping the centre of gravity as low as possible in the body; breathing deeply from the stomach; flexing the knees loosely; letting the shoulders fall heavily; complete relaxation of the head and torso which remain unaffected by the movement of the legs; keeping the head at the same level throughout; slowly rolling on the soles of the feet from the toes to the heel;

sometimes changing direction by stepping backwards; perhaps studying Tai-chi to improve the sense of placing the centre of gravity.

The same precision and commitment were displayed by Jutta Lampe in the role of Princess Natalie. In Act IV, scene IV, Natalie

13 Prinz von Homburg (Bruno Ganz) as somnambulist. The Elector (Peter Lühr) and his wife (Katharina Tüschen) look on.

brings the letter from the Elector promising a reprieve if Homburg can honestly declare his treatment unjust. Jutta Lampe entered, as excited as a child bringing a birthday gift, then, seeing that Homburg would not accept the offer of reprieve, carried her simplicity of manner to the point where it almost became simple-minded – an astonishing risk taken by the actress. When Homburg finally resolved to choose death rather than dishonour, Lampe laughed, partly with relief, partly from hysteria, kissed him briefly but tenderly and left – a telling expression of the tensions within Natalie: on the one hand the desire to save the life of the man she loved; on the other the yearning to love the man who will give his life for honour.

The role of the Elector had to be filled by someone from outside the company, since there was no one of a suitable age at the Schaubühne. The choice fell on Peter Lühr, a leading actor at the Munich Kammerspiele, whose participation was welcomed as strongly as Therese Giehse's two years previously. His Elector maintained an authoritative presence while still allowing the role to be subjected to criticism, "a cunning and cold-hearted egotist" (Hans Mayer, *Theater heute*, 1972/12, p. 12).

Once again, there was hardly a positive alternative hinted at in Stein's production. As with *Tasso* he seemed to have taken a beautiful insect and – just as beautifully – dissected it minutely, as much as to say: there, that is what is in this creature. It was yet again an exquisite and perfect operation, but one knew that the poor thing would never fly again. Apart from that luminous horizon the only glimpse of a positive future lay in the character of Kottwitz. To quote Hans Mayer again (*ibid.*, p. 14): "Otto Sander's portrayal of Kottwitz is astonishing: not a nobleman, hardly an officer; rather, a sergeant-major from peasant stock, but in his confrontation with the Elector the embodiment of a plebeian hope for the future."

In terms of Stein's development as a director, *Prinz von Homburg* had not taken him much further than the area and style he had already explored in *Tasso*. Bruno Ganz kept on asking why they were doing the play and wondered whether they were not "stagnating." Stein was irritated by Ganz's know-all attitude, and accused him of playing the part too romantically, like Gérard Philippe, "a bit of a Sonny Boy" (Protocol no. 313, 14 April 1973). Stein had wanted to work more on the physical expression of the role (as they had achieved in the "somnambulist" sequence) but Ganz began to refuse direction, often turning away when Stein spoke to him. This was undoubtedly the beginning of Ganz's drifting away from the Schaubühne towards full-time work in the cinema.

Another source of self-criticism was that the Natalie–Elector scene had been so excellent that Stein had done little work on it and that its quality had then begun to decline. Stein now recognized that it was sometimes important to analyse why a scene was working well, so that the actors might achieve a technical understanding of their performance in order to reproduce it any number of times. This was especially important with *Prinz von Homburg* which over two seasons was performed 147 times (eleven times less than Stein's most frequently performed piece, *Peer Gynt*).

Perhaps it was with the intention of challenging himself with new material that Stein next turned in the direction of comedy, which – apart from his collaboration on *Cock-a-Doodle Dandy* – he had not yet attempted. But first he had to perform a rescue operation on the parallel production to *Homburg*. This was Marieluise Fleisser's *Fegefeuer in Ingolstadt* (*Purgatory in Ingolstadt*), a *Volksstück* (play about common people) premièred in 1926 under the direction of Bertolt Brecht and Paul Bildt. Stein first proposed the play on 14 June 1971 and it was eventually agreed to invite Peter Löscher as a guest to direct it while Stein worked on *Homburg*.

Unfortunately, Peter Löscher had no special insights to offer his actors nor the ability to explore with them. Even in the casting discussions Löscher came under attack and on 28 October 1972, some six weeks after the start of rehearsals, the ensemble asked to break off work with him. On 16 November Stein took over the production, and in four weeks, delighted at the opportunity of saving the day, he knocked the production into shape. When it opened on 19 December 1972 it was hailed as yet another success.

Directors other than Stein had always suffered problems at the Schaubühne. "As far as guest directors are concerned, it seems that we are such an 'insider-group' that it is almost impossible for others to work here" (Rüdiger Hacker, Protocol no. 502, 30 November 1975). Claus Peymann, who left after disagreements with the ensemble, accused Clever and Lampe of "having a Stein fixation." It seems that Stein has set such a high standard of informed directing coupled with readiness to share problems with his actors that the ensemble is very mistrustful of either uncertain or over-confident directors. The only director to have fully won the trust of the ensemble is Klaus Michael Grüber, like Stein a protégé of Kurt Hübner's. On 14 September 1971, it was decided to invite him to join the Schaubühne and he first directed there the following year (Ödön von Horváth's *Geschichten aus dem Wiener Wald – Tales from the Vienna Woods*, premièred 18 August 1972). There followed Euripides' *Bacchae* (1973),

Hölderlin's *Empedokles* (1975) and *Winterreise* (*Winter Journey*), 1977, each of them very successful. Grüber is an excellent complement to Stein, incredibly inventive and daring (the *Winterreise* was performed in the freezing cold of the Berlin winter in the Olympic Stadium). He has a much more ritual approach to theatre and develops an imaginative conception at a much earlier stage than Stein does, and he generally regards Stein's work as pedestrian. Stein is somewhat more generous in his assessment of Grüber's work (*Die Zeit*, 2 January 1976):

There are two divergent strains in all theatre work: on the one hand there is an instinctive need for greater rationality, for greater precision, for "scientification" as Herr Brecht called it; in a totally different direction there are questions about the irrationality of what theatre represents, about its immediate "experientiality." They are two aspects of current work in the theatre which have become separated and which somehow must be brought together again. At the Schaubühne there are two directors who definitely complement each other, Klaus Michael Grüber and myself.

The comedy chosen to form Stein's next exploration of the bourgeoisie was Eugène Labiche's *La Cagnotte* (*Das Sparschwein* – *The Piggy Bank* or *Kitty*). He turned to French comedy, because he insisted that there was no comedy in German and because he could in a sense settle the long-standing desire to do a play about the Commune. Indeed the provincial bourgeoisie of 1864 who form the main characters of the piece were the complete opposite of the revolutionary *communards* – life "seen from the other side of the barricades" (unpublished interview with Bergmann, 1978) – but once again Stein was interested in working, as he put it, *"ex negativo,"* in other words, puncturing the self-image of the bourgeoisie so that it is encouraged to seek some other social role for itself.

La Cagnotte was one of the more interesting of Labiche's 175 pieces for the theatre. It tells how seven members of the provincial bourgeoisie decide to break into the kitty of their regular card games and spend the accumulated *sous* on a trip to Paris. In Paris, however, things go disastrously wrong: they are overcharged in a restaurant, are brought to justice when they cannot pay and are further accused of pick-pocketing. They escape from the police station to the marriage broker where Léonida, the middle-aged but wealthy spinster of the party, hopes to find a good match. To her dismay, she discovers that one of her unknown suitors is a member of her own party, the tedious and vain chemist Cordenbois, and, worse still, the other is the police officer they have just escaped from. In Labiche, the group flee once more, this time taking shelter on a building site and haggling over the price of a roll with a local shopkeeper. By accident a window and a basket of eggs get smashed and the situation of the penniless fugitives becomes more and more desperate until Félix, a young lawyer, appears as a kind of *deus ex machina* to pay off their debts and explain everything to the police.

In the Schaubühne version, translated and adapted by Botho Strauss, the ending was predictably changed to give the piece more political relevance. In an outburst of violence these otherwise respectable members of society physically attacked the police officer, and on the building site smashed up their immediate surroundings in order to build a barricade. As they cowered behind it, Félix walked in silhouette across the front of the stage, clutching a new piggy bank, oblivious of their presence. Here there was no rescue: the *petite bourgeoisie* was doomed. For here the political reference to contemporary events was clearly made: the building site on which they hid was a result of the demolition work initiated by Haussmann to build the broad boulevards of Paris – wide military thoroughfares that would make control of the growing plebeian population easier. This apparently so rich and established cross-section of the pro-vincial *petite bourgeoisie* found itself caught in the crossfire between the authorities and the rising proletariat and, panic-stricken and demoralized, they turned to violent anarchy to defend themselves: "A pleasure-trip to Paris, to the 'capital of the world' . . . ends with the apocalyptic vision of total financial catastrophe . . . This version emphasizes towards the end the potential for criminality and anarchy which is aroused in the respectable bourgeois when he finds himself in a state of complete destitution," (Programme, p. 56).

Thus, even where one might least expect it, in a French farce, Stein discovered and communicated political insights. To do this, while not abandoning the comedy of the situations nor the exaggeratedly drawn characters, he strived for much greater realism than is usual in playing farces. The text therefore dispensed with all asides and monologues (which were omitted or reworked in dialogue form) and with the vaudeville-style songs with which three of the acts and some of the scenes end.

Karl-Ernst Herrmann's set achieved complete photographic real-ism. The salon of the opening act was removed to expose a real street, constructed from authentic cobblestones, surrounded by stone and brickwork and overhung with the iron and glass roofing of an arcade. To one side, on white tiles, the restaurant scene was played; to the other side, beside a tall sliding iron gate, the police station was cre-ated. In the centre stood the demolition site, a row of vertical planks of varying heights. Before the group could escape behind them, water showered down from sprinklers above the stage, as realistic a rain-storm as it is possible to achieve in the theatre.

Stein seemed here to be exploring the limits of theatrical realism. It was uncharacteristic of his method to strive for such naturalism (one recalls the stuffed animals of *Peer Gynt*), and it would appear that he was here using extreme realism not to create but to destroy an illusion. He knew that the audience would not "believe" in the rain-storm, that they would be more concerned about how the effect was achieved or who would have to clear up the mess. In the context of the comedy it became part of the joke, a more refined version of the clown tipping a bucket of water over someone. So a powerful theatrical ambiguity could be established: the stage picture was as undeniably authentic as a daguerreotype and yet created that sense

14   Labiche's *Piggy Bank*. The "super-realism" of Karl-Ernst Herrmann's set.

of unreality, at once nostalgic and slightly disturbing, that one feels on seeing old photographs.

The performances also established the characters as realistic figures in a specific historical situation and yet allowed their comic behaviour to induce both laughter and a degree of sympathy. It was as though the well-to-do, top-hatted, gout-ridden figures of Chaplin's world were allowed to show that, behind their smug opulence, they too were worthy of attention. Most striking was the portrayal of Léonida by Jutta Lampe, for the first time playing an older woman instead of her usual role as a young heroine. As Volker Canaris said (*Theater heute,* 1978/13, p. 28):

This Léonida was a virtuoso achievement of theatrical transformation, which used totally external techniques to describe a thoroughly realistic character. For Lampe never turned this middle-aged spinster into a caricature. Her feelings were indeed always a size too big, her *petit bourgeois* consciousness never allowed her to become a part of the fashionable world she yearned for – and such comic incongruities were intensified by heaving her padded bosom whenever she sighed with longing, by letting her elongated nose tremble with moral indignation, by waddling with Chaplinesque legs under an outsize hooped skirt in her busy determination never to be left behind. In short: the comedy which arises when a young, clever and beautiful woman plays a stupid old maid was fully exploited – and yet the character retained dignity and a certain humanity which inspired a considerable amount of sympathy in the midst of ridicule.

Stein's exploration of bourgeois realism was to be pursued over a year later in Gorky's *Summerfolk,* but first he was to confront quite different forms of theatre. Meanwhile, in drawing a balance of his work on the nineteenth century, he said in *Der Abend* on 27 August that the repeated theme of all these plays was the examination of "the relationship between the individual and the collective" which remained undefined and which was to be "examined and discussed in our work." The pursuit of this exploration next led him to the earliest form of Western theatre, to that of Ancient Greece.

On 6 January 1973, it was decided that Grüber would direct *The Bacchae* and that, under Stein's direction, the lengthy discussions and research in preparation for the production would not be relegated to essays and notes in the programme but would be presented in a theatrical form to the public. At this stage Stein already pointed to the difficulties of such a presentation (Protocol no. 284): "We shall have to be clear in our own minds that very little of our preparation will be capable of being transferred to the stage and that very little can be communicated for or about the world of today."

When preparatory work began at the end of June 1973, Sturm and Stein again steered the ensemble away from a too narrowly political approach to the material. Frazer and Graves were recommended as reading matter, for "with the investigation of man's relationship with Nature we find ourselves in the deepest origins of history" (Dieter Sturm, Protocol no. 332, 30 July 1973). The major problem was that before Aeschylus there were no extant texts for performance and that only the most fragmentary evidence existed about the origins of Greek theatre. For this reason, Stein argued, the ensemble could not rely on material being prepared by the director and *Dramaturg* but would have to collaborate in creating their own programme: "We must arrive at a form of presentation that is understood by everyone in completely the same way" (Stein, Protocol no. 284).

That summer the ensemble chartered a boat to the Mediterranean to visit the principal sites of Ancient Greece. The trip was paid for by the actors themselves, and the same sort of practical research was later undertaken in Russia for the *Summerfolk* production and in England by fifteen members of the Shakespeare ensemble. It was a sign of the serious commitment of the company that at their own expense and in their vacation they should elect to remain together to continue work on a project. The Greek trip also lent interesting insights into the differences between Stein and Grüber: on the Acropolis, Stein, guide-book in hand, was engaged in reading about the historical details of the Parthenon and communicating them to anyone who cared to listen; meanwhile Grüber was wandering aimlessly amongst the ruins, enthusing about the shapes and colours of the masonry in the bright sunlight.

That October, at the third general discussion about the *Antiquity Project*, Stein proposed that one way into the obscure origins of theatre was to draw parallels between basic forms of ritual and the experience of acting. It was important to remember, he said, "that a theatrical representation always contains within it the quality of creating something impossible, something that seemingly cannot be created . . . One might for example say that theatre was invented only in order to conjure away death" (Protocol no. 358, undated).

The first evening of the *Antiquity Project*, which opened on 6 February 1974 under Stein's direction, did not therefore present any attempt at archaeological reconstruction of early forms of the theatre but demonstrated simply the relationship between the actor and his body both in a theatrical and a ritual context. As the introductory remarks of the programme stated:

We were of the opinion that we could not perform a play like *The Bacchae* without an introduction or a preparatory evening. At first we planned to present the research of our group perhaps in the form of a theatrical museum [This form was indeed later adopted in *Shakespeare's Memory*]. Later we wanted to show the original relationship between man and nature, to show the emergence of human consciousness, of division of labour, of language etc. This was all beyond our reach, because there was no suitable text. There remained only questions about our craft, whose methods had somehow developed from Greek theatre. Ritual enactment and tragic performance on the one hand, our craft as actors on the other. Are there connections? Not surprisingly we arrived at an examination of the lowest common denominator: the use of the human body as a means of representation . . . In spite of many reservations we now believe that demonstrating this first step is the only kind of theatrical introduction to a Greek tragedy which we can justify.

For the first time at the Schaubühne – apart from the touring productions of the Workers' Theatre – a production was designed for a space outside the theatre. *Peer Gynt* had, after a run at the Schaubühne, been transferred to an exhibition hall, but primarily because this doubled the seating capacity. Now, however, Grüber in particular felt constrained by the limitations of the Schaubühne building itself. In this frustration could be seen the beginnings of the pressure to move to a bigger, purpose-built theatre.

For the *Antiquity Project* an exhibition hall was again hired. This in no way reduced the Schaubühne company's ability to attract capacity audiences: its reputation was now so great that its audiences would follow it to any corner of Berlin – to Spandau for Shakespeare, to the Olympia Stadium for Hölderlin. As Stein points out, no other theatre in the world could depend on such loyalty.

For the first evening, entitled *Exercises for Actors*, the floor of the hall, strewn with sand, had depressions containing benches for the spectators, so that they sat in six different areas just below the level of the performing area surrounding them. The way into the hall led past the room in which the actors could be observed making up their faces in the style of Greek actors portrayed on vases. From the roof of the hall hung a massive clock, and the time was announced at regular intervals, so that the actors, once more free of their grease paint, could take their places and begin their exercises together without further signal. The initial series of exercises were the stock-in-trade of any properly trained actor: breathing, listening, walking, exploring movement of the limbs, facial expressions, contraction and release. In order to make the experience more theatrical, sound effects were added: an aeroplane overhead which the actors followed in their imagination; a baby crying, as the actors explored seizing things with their hands. This all had something of the tedium of watching an orchestra tune their instruments, but at least, in contrast with groups like Living Theatre, it was presented as an honest demonstration not as some profound experience in which the audience were expected to share.

The next section, "The Hunt," had a more obviously theatrical quality and gave a strong awareness to the actors of "the bloody seriousness and the dangers associated with the origins of our ridiculous profession" (Programme note). While some actors raked the sand, others strapped a "Victim" (Heinrich Giskes) into a heavily padded costume which protected his torso and thighs and gave him the appearance of a huge bug, like an image from Kafka. Two other actors, dressed like American gangsters in long white mackintoshes, trilbies and dark glasses, and armed with large knives, began to

15   *Antiquity Project.* "The Hunt."

search for the Victim, who was at first "protected" by the chorus kneeling around him. When he was sighted, the chase commenced to the excited panting of the chorus. At first the chorus tried to hinder the hunters, but gradually their mood changed and they then encouraged the pursuit with bestial sounds and spasms of the body. It occurred to me to wonder what might have happened, had the public been sufficiently disturbed by the sight of these gangster figures hunting down this terrified half-human creature to intervene in the chase themselves. It was most unlikely, however, since German audiences have a great sense of propriety; for as Lenin once remarked, if Germans decided to storm a railway station, they would all buy platform tickets first. As Stein himself commented: "The chase was staged in such a way that the audience were interested in the way it developed. 'Wanting to save' the Victim would have been totally inappropriate. Only once did a drunk intervene in the performance" (personal communication, 18 October 1980).

The Victim was eventually pursued into a mud bath and, as he stumbled away exhausted, was stabbed in the padded breast by one of the hunters. The chorus began a lament but were soon incited to join in the chase of the now "wounded" creature, who was finally encircled and slit open with the knives. The chorus plunged their hands into the open "wounds" and smeared themselves with "blood" to the sound of primitive horn music. Then, slowly, stillness and recognition of what they had done returned to the group and they covered up the traces of the killing.

This primitive chase and the subsequent disillusionment were clearly excellent preparations for the dismemberment of Pentheus in *The Bacchae* and especially the part played in this by his mother, Agave (Edith Clever). But such improvisational preparation was hardly worthy of inclusion in a public performance. Here, as with the rest of the programme, the Schaubühne ensemble were clearly depending on the reputation they had established for themselves. The same sequence performed equally well by an unknown student group would have been dismissed as mere self-indulgence.

The next sequence involved the introduction of a "Sacrificial Object," a large cylindrical affair constructed from animal skulls and bones around which the chorus danced primitive dances, wound strands of wool and chanted the "Hymn to Helios" of Mesomedes.

In the interval Michael König wearing an impressive phallus leapt around as a satyr in the so-called "summer garden," though at this time of the year usually under snow. As the audience returned, they were divided up according to sex and obediently followed instructions to sit on separate sides of the room. On the male side three actors, and on the female side three actresses were stripped naked for the "Initiation." They were pulled and pushed and tossed in the air in variants of the trust games familiar to most theatre students. The naked bodies were then buried in the sand, uncovered, smeared with kaolin, flour and black dust and their heads decorated like crude masks. These weird distortions of the human figure were then shown how to walk, seize hold of things and see, and were finally re-integrated into the group in a collective embrace.

Now a sliding wall moved slowly the length of the whole area driving the male and female spectators together and obliging them to enter an adjoining area where Eberhard Feik recited Prometheus' monologue (ascribed to Aeschylus), in which Prometheus tells of the growth of the human consciousness ending with the line "From me, Prometheus, come the skills of all mankind." As he delivered this speech, he was gradually immured by being plastered into a wall. The evening had therefore shown the development from basic body-exploration through ritual to one of the earliest extant texts of dramatic literature and in the final image suggested a serious reflection

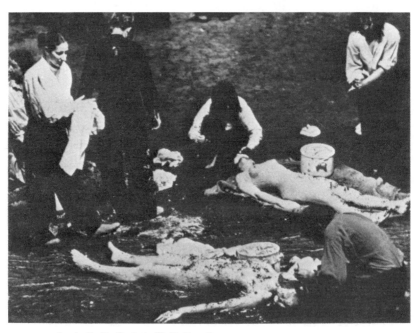

16   *Antiquity Project.* "Initiation."

on man's emergence from his primitive state of unselfconscious behaviour: the gifts of Prometheus are also the source of suffering.

Undoubtedly, the exercises and improvisatory work which formed the content of the programme were of great value to the ensemble in preparing for Grüber's production of *The Bacchae*. Whether they were sufficient in themselves to form a public performance is another matter. As Reinhard Baumgart wrote in the *Süddeutsche Zeitung*, 16–17 February 1974: "The tirelessly researched introversion of this group has something of the sense of a mystery play for initiates. The audience are asked to leave themselves in the cloakroom." From the left came particularly strong attacks. The critics of the German Democratic Republic, who had sometimes given Stein a favourable mention, denounced this undertaking as "madhouse theatre." Stein, however, insisted that the first evening of the *Antiquity Project* was "every bit as political as *The Mother*" (*Die Zeit*, 2 January 1976). In intention, with its desire to investigate basic social forms, it was undoubtedly a political undertaking. In its execution, though, it was merely a somewhat pretentious demonstration of acting exercises, better relegated to the rehearsal room.

With characteristically frank self-criticism Stein stated a year later (Protocol no. 470, 30 April 1975) that the *Antiquity Project* was "inexcusable. They had not been able to transpose for performance the material that had fascinated them in their preparatory work for the project. They merely demonstrated the kind of exercises an actor normally performs before going on stage." The chief benefit from the *Antiquity Project* was to come later: in the much more theatrical format of *Shakespeare's Memory*.

It was now becoming a pattern in Stein's work that, after a major undertaking like the *Antiquity Project*, he would turn to a less demanding production. Shortly after Peymann's departure in February 1971, Stein declared he would have directed a play of the quality of Handke's *Ride over Lake Constance* in two weeks (Protocol no. 90, 14 February 1971). In October of 1973 it was agreed that he would direct Handke's latest piece, *Die Unvernünftigen sterben aus* (*They Are Dying Out*). The theme of the play as described by Stein (Protocol no. 354, undated) was "capitalist reality as seen by a highly developed bourgeois writer, described in figures and episodes . . . which are only fragments and reflections of Handke's way of seeing things." The central figure of the piece is a rich businessman, Herr Quitt, who renegues on a deal made with his colleagues, strangles a troublesome shareholder and finally kills himself by ramming his head against a rock. There is some implication in all this that the arbitrary wielding of power by capitalism will lead inevitably to its own destruction, but Handke is not making any particularly clear political point: he merely creates a theatrical image of contemporary capitalism, an image that contains neither the recognizable situation of a realistic piece nor the autonomous world of absurdist theatre. This was the first contemporary piece Stein had directed at the Schaubühne (with the peripheral exception of Kelling's *The Altercation*), and it seems that his interest in it was to some extent conditioned by his desire to show that he could excel in this area too, if he chose to. In his approach he did not try to squeeze things out of the play that were not there. Whereas all his other productions had involved free adaptations of the original, he now resolved to follow all the stage directions, including those for the set, which Klaus Weiffenbach designed. This was a significant decision and a reasonable one: if a director alters the text of a classic like Goethe's *Tasso* or Kleist's *Prinz von Homburg*, then the original is still there as common cultural property; the director has endangered nothing except his own reputation. But in a case like Handke, for most of the Berlin audience this would be their only opportunity to become acquainted with *They Are Dying Out*, and the director has the responsibility "to leave the play as it is" (Stein, Protocol no. 432, 18 November 1974). So one arrives at the paradox that a director needs to show greater humility before a new play of unproven worth than before one of the masterpieces of world theatre.

Generally, therefore, Stein worked, as he often does, "from sentence to sentence," clarifying, rendering more plausible, not necessarily on a psychological level, but in terms of certain representative figures within a given situation. Bruno Ganz's portrayal of Quitt maintained a sad aggressiveness which made his suicidal act seem totally consequent. The three manager friends of Quitt were all differentiated as types: from the lyrical manner of Koerber-Kent (Rüdiger Hacker) to the upper-class superciliousness of von Wullnow (Otto Sander) and the duodenal anxiety of Lutz (Werner Rehm).

Stein's direction was determined by a pursuit of clarity rather than of psychological realism. Indeed, he originally intended that for parts of the play the stage should be screened off by a wall that would be partly transparent, partly a mirror, so that the audience would become aware of their own "reflection" on stage. The voices of the actors would have been amplified by the use of microphones. This idea had to be dropped because of the technical difficulties, but it indicates clearly that Stein was intent on preserving the theatrical

distance of the action. As Gerd Jäger wrote of Stein's production
(*Theater heute*, 1974/7, p. 34):

Stein clarifies. He does not offer interpretations. He attempts to transfer
Handke's text to the stage. And only here, by creating distance, does Stein
help us to understand what Handke means by: "It suddenly occurs to me
that I am performing something that isn't there, and that is the difference."
The difference between theatre and reality. It's worth preserving.

Stein's was the sixth production of the play on German-language
stages. Handke, on the occasion of the *Tasso* performance in Frankfurt, had written a strong attack on Stein. Now he hailed Stein's production of *They Are Dying Out* as the "most decisive realization to
date" (quoted in Iden, p. 116). For most critics it was the definitive
reading of the play, and, significantly, it has hardly been performed
since. It is after all difficult to match oneself against the quality of the
Schaubühne, even when Stein is operating in unfamiliar territory.

The next challenge he took on was to explore an area of theatre
which he had deliberately avoided until now – the portrayal of psychological realism. For Stein, and here he again revealed the influence of Brecht's thinking, psychological realism was a dangerous
reinforcement of the bourgeois concept of the individual. The need
was to show characters as representatives of their social situation and
– in plays as various as *Tasso, Peer Gynt* and the Handke piece – this
is exactly what Stein achieved. He had, however, never applied
Brecht's ideas crudely and was always strongly aware of the psychological dimension of a character, while keeping this in the background and not allowing subtleties of motivation to obscure the central idea. Now it seemed that Stein was so totally in command of his
art that he could risk a new level of psychological complexity without
abandoning the clarity he regarded as essential.

The play chosen for this project was Gorky's *Datshniki,* a title referring to the middle-class custom in pre-revolutionary Russia of leav-
ing the city to spend the summer in a rented villa or *datsha* in the
country. The title in German is usually *Sommergäste* ("summer-
guests"); in English it has been variously translated as *Summerfolk* or
Vacationers. This play completed for Stein a cycle of plays on the Russian Revolution: *Optimistic Tragedy* dealt with the civil war following
the Revolution of 1917; *The Mother* had traced events from the first
uprisings of 1905 to 1917; now as a prelude to these upheavals, stood
Gorky's play, written in 1904, in which he shows a cross-section of
the *petite bourgeoisie,* some doomed, some on their way to discover-
ing a new role in society.

The *datshniki* are thirteen professionals (lawyers, doctors, engineer, writer, etc.) who have met at the summer residence of Bassov, a somewhat unscrupulous lawyer. Most of them, while desultorily pursuing their professions, find themselves in a situation of idleness which is filled with aimless pastimes, empty love-affairs and trivial quarrels. It is a world not far removed from that of Chekhov, but the major difference is that here Gorky has included an undeniably positive character. Maria Lvovna, a 35-year-old doctor, is independent, self-sufficient and filled with social concern. It is she who diagnoses the sickness from which the *datshniki* are suffering (Act IV, translated from the Schaubühne version, Programme, p. 35):

We must change ourselves completely, yes. All of us – who are we? The children of washerwomen, cooks, workers. And what do we do? We die of boredom and weariness . . . It's not right. There have never before in this country been so many educated people that have come from the masses. Have we forgotten the drudgery of their lives, how, day in day out, they almost suffocate in darkness and filth – and they are our blood-relations! . . . We must help them, but not from pity, not because we are sorry for them – we must do it for our own sakes! So that we aren't paralysed to death in this accursed isolation, so that we don't get giddy when we look into the chasm that separates us from them . . . They sent us on ahead, so that we could discover the way towards a better life for them. But we have left them behind, we have lost them and have strayed into a wilderness, where we only watch each other inwardly destroyed by nervous tension. Yes, I believe that is the reason for all our emotional scenes. We have brought them upon us and we deserve to suffer. We have no right to complain.

It is also Maria Lvovna who finally induces Bassov's wife, Varvara, and her brother, Vlas, to escape with two other *datshniki* from their empty existence to a new and purposeful life in the city. The five proto-revolutionaries leave behind the others who are too frightened or too smug to risk the change that Maria Lvovna demands of them. At the end Shalimov, the writer, reassures Bassov: "It's all so meaningless – people and what happens to them, it means nothing . . . Pour me some more wine . . . none of it makes any difference, dear fellow." But throughout the play have been heard the rattles and whistles of the watchmen doing their rounds of the estate, and within two decades those warning sounds will have shown what a vast difference human activity could make.

The decision to go ahead with a production of the play, which had already, on 19 November 1972, been proposed for the programme, was now prompted by the news that the Sender Freies Berlin broadcasting company might finance the making of a film with the Schaubühne ensemble. Stein, whose only previous attempt at making a film, *Saved* in 1967, had been a failure, but who had always had ambitions in this medium, seized upon this opportunity. The Schau-bühne needed the money, and it was just the sort of creative challenge that Stein welcomed. He and Botho Strauss therefore began work on a film-script adaptation of Gorky's *Summerfolk,* and much of the presentation of the theatre version retained cinematic qualities, especially in its cross-cutting from one group of actors to another. Gorky's play, which he subtitled "Scenes," follows a conventional dramaturgy, in which characters enter to conduct their dialogue and exit when they have had their say. The Stein–Strauss adaptation showed the group almost all present on stage for the length of the play. Not only did this create the cinematic montage effect which Stein first explored in *Tasso* and was to employ again successfully in the opening section of *As You Like It;* it also was very appropriate as a means of portraying the *datshniki,* their idleness, their mutual dependence, and their sense of being imprisoned together: "Their inability to escape from each other must in Stein's view lie in the characters themselves and not be clarified by constant exits and entrances" (Protocol, 30 September 1974). When work began on the production in September 1974, the television company was not yet ready to release funds. Stein insisted that they should nevertheless go ahead with a theatre production, even though the financial situation of the Schaubühne was precarious. Preparations therefore began on the usual lines: Stanislavsky was recommended as essential reading, Stein delivered a paper on Gorky, Sturm contributed one on nineteenth-century Russian literature. That summer they had all visited the USSR in preparation for the project. The casting discussions between the artistic staff and the actors achieved agreement on all the major parts: Wolf Redl as Bassov, Edith Clever as Varvara, Jutta Lampe as Maria Lvovna, Bruno Ganz as Shalimov. The only exception was the role of Vlas, the anarchic, clown-like mocker of his fellows. Nineteen of the twenty actors present voted in favour of Gerd David, who had first appeared as an old costermonger in *The Piggy Bank* and who, it seemed to the other actors, at last deserved a substantial role. The artistic staff were in favour of Michael König having the part, and Stein argued his case strongly. Over three years earlier, with reference to *Peer Gynt,* Stein had contended that there must be limitations to the democratic process of casting: "the allocation of roles cannot be totally democratic. Only the expression of [Stein's] views can be subjected to a democratic process, in which his views are explained and criticized. But he can't democratize his ideas of what someone is capable of and what someone is not capable of" (quoted by Elfriede Irrall, undated circular, 1972). Now there was the possibility of a confrontation: the actors (and – with customary selflessness – König amongst them) were concerned that one of their number should be "given a break." Stein could not see how David could cope with the role. Theoretically the actors could have insisted that Stein accept their decision, but in practice no cast that has any respect for its director would force him or her into unwillingly working with someone. König was therefore given the part, and David, until he left in 1978, continued to play only minor roles in Stein's productions.

The adaptation of Gorky's text required a considerable rewriting of the first two acts to maintain the presence of all the *datshniki* on stage together, for in the original they do not come together until the picnic in Act III. In addition, Maria Lvovna's daughter, who in Gorky is a too-good-to-be-true figure, was omitted; in the Schaubühne version she was referred to as being at a boarding school. Not only did this dispense with the awkwardness of a not wholly credible character and economize on her part and that of her boyfriend; it also prevented Maria Lvovna from becoming too idealized. Although she displayed an active social conscience, she had a remunerative private practice as a doctor and sent her daughter to a private school. As with Stein himself, her political stance was well subsidized.

A similarly complex treatment was accorded to the "optimistic" ending. As Maria Lvovna and her four followers left for a new future, they broke out of the thicket fence that surrounded the *datsha* garden. But their escape was clumsy, and Varvara, far from revealing great heroic energy, stumbled wearily onwards supported by the others. Their spontaneous "vote against fear, against timidity, against thinking everything over ten times" (Stein, *Der Spiegel*, 2 February 1976) was unquestionably a positive move but not an unproblematic one.

The thicket and live birch trees in genuine soil which formed the rear of the stage acted therefore as a restraining barrier out of which the progressive characters had to escape. ("Sometimes I suddenly have the feeling that I'm trapped in a prison," said Varvara in Act II, Programme, p. 20). The simultaneous presence of all the characters, sometimes in interior scenes, created difficulties in finding an appropriate set-design. Initially, Stein had considered creating a *datsha* garden in an exhibition hall with the audience moving from one group of actors to another as the focus shifted. On a conventional stage the main problem was the siting of the *datsha*. If it were at the back, there would be a loss of intimacy with the actors in the interior scenes; if at the front, the same would be true of the outdoor scenes.

17 Gorky's *Summerfolk*. The *datsha* in the foreground with meadow
and trees beyond. Kaleriya (Ilse Ritter) recites while a worker looks on
in puzzlement.

The designer, Karl-Ernst Herrmann, hit upon an ingenious solution
(Protocol, 30 September 1974):

Since their starting-point is to tell the story of a group . . . they propose to
structure the stage, so that it arises out of the groups being together, staying
together, organizing things together. The idea is to construct a platform
across the front of the stage, representing the terrace of the *datsha*. Behind
this platform there would be a slope representing a meadow, so that you
look out of the house into the country. The sides and rear of the stage should
be cage-like, so that there is an enclosed area where people meet and from
which they basically cannot escape. For the scenes in the house, the assump-
tion is made that they are played after dark, so that with the help of lighting
an interior scene can be created.

   In acting style this play represented Stein's first approach to true
naturalism since *Saved*. Until now there had been three characteris-
tics which distinguished his deliberately artificial style. First, there
had always been a very clear focus in any given scene. Now, in *Summerfolk*, while a certain focus was maintained on the actors speaking,
part of the delight of the performance was to let the eyes wander over
the silent activities of the other performers. The critic Friedrich Luft
saw the production three times and felt he had seen three different
plays. Secondly, Stein's actors had excelled in their economy, their
plakativ style of precise and strongly projected moves and gestures.
Now they were required to elaborate, to seek for detail for no other

reason than that it was lifelike. Thirdly, the Schaubühne actors had regularly arrived at fixed and polished performances in which every intention and gesture would be exactly repeated. Here, while discipline would not permit any free improvisation, the actors had more autonomy than ever in developing their performances. For them, as well, no two performances were quite the same.

As the first page of the programme states: "The production offers the chance of getting to know a group of people just as you get to know real people in a society where the most fleeting contact calls forth stubborn assumptions and fantasies about them." The fleeting contact was not established only by dialogue but also by the many activities the group were involved in – a constantly changing picture of the busy pursuit of leisure. Stein's own rough notes indicate the range of ideas explored by the ensemble, almost all of which were used in performance:

Leisure activities	*Work*
Communal eating of lunch, dinner	Writing
Tea ceremony	Reading documents
Recitation to music	Domestic duties –
Play rehearsal	drawing curtains
Reading books/newspapers	rearranging furniture
Singing together	tidying up
Playing an instrument	Medical activities
Looking at nature (terrace, pavilion)	Engineer's activities?
Getting fishing rod ready	Kropilkin's work
Picnic	Counting (?who?) Plans
Walking	Administration
Drinking	
Smoking	
Business with clothing	
Sexual intercourse	
Playing chess	
Handing out sweets	
Swimming	
Acting in a play	
Boat trip	

The psychological realism of the performances depended on clear insights by the actors. In the case of Olga (Sabine Andreas), a programme note shows the subtlety of approach which Stein used in his direction: "Olga's self-hatred is an extreme bid for attention and tenderness and yet at the same time the most certain means of destroying any contact. Inevitably one finally shares the disgust which someone like that feels for herself" (Programme, p. 15). Similarly, the ability of Varvara to free herself from her intolerable existence did not proceed from a steady growth of frustration. Indeed, at the end of the picnic scene in Act III she was more tender to her husband than ever before: "The process of her becoming free should be as ponderous and as contradictory as possible" (Programme, p. 30).

It would be a mistake to assume, however, that Stein had here turned to a completely Stanislavskian search for stage realism. The opening programme note stated that the realism of the play "arises more from debate than from the psychology of the individual character." Where this debate demanded a clarity that went beyond mere representation, Stein abandoned the illusion he had been at such pains to create. So in Act I, when Varvara spoke her central speech beginning: "I don't know . . . I can't express myself very well . . . but I feel very strongly that people must change" (Programme, p. 10), Edith Clever turned to face the audience and positioned herself exactly in the middle of the stage to deliver her lines. Similarly, the threatening sounds of the watchmen and the enclosing thicket had a symbolic function which went far beyond realism.

There were moments of the play too where the characters seemed to enter a dream-world. At the end of the picnic scene, a diffused, uncanny white light played in the upper leaves of the birch trees, and the group of *datshniki* moved forward silhouetted against the light like children lost in a forest, as though they had suddenly found themselves on a planet that was no longer their own. Again, in Act IV, the group was engaged in one of their repeated altercations, when the two watchmen appeared in the background. The group froze in their various poses, while the watchmen gave a commentary on their behaviour (Programme, p. 35):

KROPILKIN. What are they up to?
PUSTOBAIKA. They're arguing. They always argue before dinner.
KROPILKIN. They've all got enough to eat. They don't need to argue.
PUSTOBAIKA. They're not arguing about dinner, they're arguing before dinner.

This scene of the ludicrous *petite bourgeoisie* suddenly frozen into their state of self-destructive aggression while the healthy proletarians looked on with detachment had all the quality of a dream, and yet it said more about the real existence of these people than any amount of subtly judged psychological nuances would have done.

Summerfolk was hailed as a triumph and generally regarded as Stein's best work since *Peer Gynt*. Friedrich Luft in his weekly review on Berlin radio on 5 January 1975 enthused: "Something took place here, which in the theatre happens only half a dozen times in one's

18   Gorky's *Summerfolk*. The *datshniki* at the end of their picnic "like children lost in the forest."

life." The play ran for 135 performances at the Schaubühne and was toured to Switzerland, Yugoslavia, France, Belgium, Finland and Russia. It was also taken to the National Theatre in London (3 to 12 March 1977) as the National's first foreign-language production. Here Stein was amused to see how differently subsidies had been apportioned compared with the Schaubühne: "We have bigger stages and smaller foyers" (Personal communication, 7 December 1977). His meticulousness surprised the National technicians: trees from Epping Forest were carefully selected and planted on stage in exactly prescribed places; before each performance the earth was watered so that it had just the right colour tone. With the exceptions of Michael Billington in *The Guardian* and David Zane Mairowitz in

Plays and Players, (vol. 24, no. 8 (1977) 18–21) English critics seemed at a loss to say anything significant about a production which, even given that it was in an "unintelligible" foreign language, was visually of a standard unequalled by anything in London for years. As Gertrud Mander reported under the headline "The best is always boring" in the *Stuttgarter Zeitung* (21 March 1977):

Characteristically all the theatre critics of the Sunday papers gave a lengthy discussion of two current sex farces before they got round to the serious (i.e. German) theatre with Stein's guest production. Briefly and often without much understanding, they awarded it a first-class mark but in the way you are obliged to give high marks to the boring pupil at the top of the class, because he is unquestionably better but not nearly so popular and amusing as the others.

A similar thing happened to the Berliner Ensemble on its first visit to London in 1956, which people now remember nostalgically, although at the time they sarcastically criticized the slow pacing and aesthetic theories. The English critics (and public?) are simply incapable of understanding the style of German theatre.

Having achieved considerable success with *Summerfolk* Stein gave up directing for the theatre for almost two years (1975–6). This was partly in order to give other directors a chance at the Schaubühne, but also to "recharge his batteries" by attempting work in new areas. In 1975 he worked on the film version of *Summerfolk*. It was not a great success amongst film critics, mainly because Stein with customary integrity had not rushed into using cinematic techniques with which he was unfamiliar: "I'm not very good at taking risks; I am very cautious in what I take on. I don't see why you have to bowl people over with your ideas. It's not my style, although I admire others who just let go, but I've got a different mentality" (*Der Tagesspiegel*, 12 October 1975). Instead of highly original ideas Stein depended on a strong acting style in his film: "I do not believe that the screen suffers from intensity of acting. I know that I will be contradicted, but I think we must explore what is possible in terms of expressiveness and strongly projected performances. We ought to push hard in that direction rather than be too half-hearted" (*Die Zeit*, 6 February 1976).

While the *Summerfolk* film represented only a minor success, his other major venture was an unequivocal failure. In November 1976 he directed Wagner's *Ring of the Nibelungen* for the Paris Opera. There had already been difficulties at an early stage, since there had been requests for Stein to clarify his conception in advance. But, as he insisted, "Theatre is a process of exploration during rehearsals. The conception is formulated by the opening night, not a year before rehearsals begin" (*Stuttgarter Zeitung*, 14 February 1975). Anyone who wishes to understand better why a director like Stein should fail in a conventional opera house need only read the relevant section of the chapter on "Deadly Theatre" in Peter Brook's *The Empty Space.*

Older, wiser, and somewhat chastened, Stein eventually returned to the Schaubühne late in 1976 to grapple with the theatrical giant of all time, Shakespeare. This too, as we shall see, was to prove a difficult experience, and his last two productions prior to the *Oresteia* project – both of plays by Botho Strauss – were once again concerned with the malaise of bourgeois society, with the contemporary manifestation of the "German misery."

Botho Strauss had worked as *Dramaturg* with Stein on *Peer Gynt, Prinz von Homburg, The Piggy Bank* (also as translator) and *Summerfolk*. His first play *Die Hypochonder* (*The Hypochondriacs*) had been premièred by Claus Peymann in Hamburg in 1972 and was then directed by Wilfried Minks at the Schaubühne in the following year. *Trilogie des Wiedersehens* (*Trilogy of Return* – literally of "seeing again," i.e. a renewed meeting and a second look) was his third play and had already been produced three times before it opened at the Schaubühne on 21 March 1978. It can hardly be claimed therefore that the Schaubühne launched the career of Strauss as a playwright; on the other hand his collaboration with Stein undoubtedly gave him insights and encouragement which have shaped the style of his writing.

In particular, in the two pieces Stein has directed, *Trilogie des Wiedersehens* and *Gross und klein* (*Great and Small*), Strauss reveals the powerful combination of realistic detail with a wider social perspective which characterizes Stein's direction. For Stein, both plays allowed him to gather strength before his next major project on *The Oresteia*. For one thing there was no necessity of painstaking preparation for *Trilogy of Return*: "Read it once, then off you go – why bother with more?" (unpublished Bergmann interview, 1978). The play depended on the accurate portrayal of contemporary West German types: Moritz, the director of an art gallery, his would-be mistress, the 42-year-old Susanne, a doctor and his alcoholic wife, an actor who has not made it and one who is past it, a failed painter and her salesman boyfriend, a printer, an author and so on. In Strauss's play these characters meet in a series of short scenes, separated like snapshots by blackouts, in one of the exhibition rooms of the gallery. Peter Stein once more used the principle of simultaneity that he had adopted for *Summerfolk*: the characters wandered in and out, sat around preoccupied with their own problems and obsessions, while scenes, in the emotional as well as the theatrical sense, were played out in their midst.

The audience, too, in Stein's production became participants in this self-contemplation of the cultured bourgeoisie. Even before the play started, some members of the audience had their photographs taken in the foyer or theatre restaurant by the youngest actor, a boy of eleven. These Polaroid prints could then be inserted into a prepared slot on the front page of the programme, suggesting that the members of the audience had also been invited to the *vernissage* of the exhibition of "Capitalist realism." Karl-Ernst Herrmann's set was hardly a set at all: one corner of the auditorium was furnished as an office, that of Moritz, the gallery director. The rest of the auditorium was filled with raked seating at right angles. The concept of a "stage" had virtually disappeared: the audience looked down on a real room.

The people in the room were also imbued with a strong sense of credibility. The programme, in place of the usual historical documentation, contained photographs and brief biographies of each of the sixteen characters, and this summary of the "given circumstances" of each role was characteristic of the clearly thought-out, realistic playing of the actors. As Libgart Schwarz, who played the main part of Susanne, said: "Acting is always a matter of recollection. And in this role I can recall many situations from my own life. I risk showing that, but it has nothing to do with exhibitionism. Acting should not be something private but something personal which affects a lot of people" (*Theater heute*, 1978/13, p. 22). Yet, and especially in Libgart Schwarz's case, the given circumstances and emotional memory did not limit the actor to the narrow path of conventional naturalism. In her portrayal of Susanne, Libgart Schwarz remained credible yet full of artifice, quite unpredictable yet clearly in command of her technical resources. Of her performance more than any other were Hellmuth Karasek's words a fitting comment: "Stein's actors are close to the audience and yet seem to be acting behind glass. Botho Strauss proceeds from the feeling that there are only second-hand feelings left. The Berlin production reflects this" (*Der Spiegel*, 3 April 1978). Schwarz, like Ulrich Wildgruber an individualistic and difficult actor, who kept on "drying" right up to the dress rehearsal, offered an astonishing sense of immediacy and yet of "acting behind glass": she adopted a curious, affected accent, she sought for phrases, pausing and gesticulating when they failed to come, she squeezed her eyes shut, whether in an attempt to concentrate or to forget it was impossible to say. She went beyond the limits

of what one expects from realistic acting to an intensity of characterization that made one feel that Schwarz had not merely brought one
of Strauss's characters to life but had created a virtually autonomous
personality, such as one might perhaps meet at the next Berlin *vernissage*.

The same extension of realism into an area where disturbingly
haunting images seemed to develop a reality beyond the theatrical
moment occurred at several points in the play. The first appears in
the stage directions as follows (*Trilogie des Wiedersehens*, Hanser,
Munich, 1976, p. 15):

All the visitors to the exhibition, that is all Moritz's friends apart from himself, stand like a chorus in the background and listen to Susanne. Bright
light.

The effect was like an image from a dream, each element of reality
recognizable in detail but in a juxtaposition that seemed unreal. The
same was true of the final image: Peter Fitz as Moritz symbolizing
his withdrawal from his surroundings by winding white adhesive
tape like a bandage round his head, covering eyes, ears, nose and
mouth.

The extreme commitment of an actress to her role was also revealed
in Stein's next production, which he subsequently filmed, the world
première of Botho Strauss's fourth play *Gross und klein* (*Great and
Small*) which opened on 8 December 1978. Edith Clever, who had
returned to the Schaubühne for *Trilogy of Return* after an absence of
almost three years, performed the lead role of Lotte, a woman in her
mid thirties, separated from her husband, searching desperately for
contact in a world fallen prey to isolation and sterility. In the first
scene she summarized her predicament and that of the world about
her: "It's all very simple: nothing goes right" (*Gross und klein*, Hanser, Munich, 1978, p. 11). In ten scenes, which Stein's production
presented faithfully over almost five hours, Lotte moved through the
desolate landscape of West German consumer society, from the dismal package tour to Morocco, to the loneliness of a tenement house
and to the final scene of Lotte alone, her hair white, her clothing
faded, in the antiseptic brilliance of an out-patients' waiting room.
Edith Clever sustained this remarkable journey through the ten sta-
tions with impressive range and variety of expression. The most
intense moment came in the symbolic seventh scene, "Wrong number," when, her mascara running in a clown-like streak below each
eye, she fell into hysterical despair over the blank pages of the book
of her life: she used the book to smash a chair, and blood began to
run from its pages. This expressionist image seemed to imply that

although she had destroyed the symbol of settled living, there was yet no release, and her suffering had to continue.

For this production Stein and his designer, Karl-Ernst Herrmann, used the film studios where *As You Like It* was staged. Horseshoe-shaped seating was erected for the spectators, who looked down on a stage, the many transformations of which were achieved by twelve-metre tall curtains opening and closing. The electric motors responsible for these changes initially proved inadequate, and the première had to be delayed twice. The curtains also lent a curiously artificial framework to scenes of otherwise total realism. Their most effective use was in the final scene, where white curtains surrounded the audience and action in an unbroken circle, reflecting the sterility of the waiting room: like Lotte, the audience were patients suffering from a disease for which they would wait in vain to be treated. The only theatrical reasons for using the film studio, it seemed, were to facilitate the complex transformation of scenes and to permit sufficient space for the central scene to take place. This scene, entitled "Ten rooms," shows sixteen episodes of life in a tenement house. In Strauss's text there is some ambiguity whether each room is a different room or whether it is always the same room with a different

19 Strauss's *Great and Small*. The "eight room" scene.

occupant. In Stein's production this ambiguity was resolved by presenting eight rooms in a two-storey arrangement, reminiscent of the simultaneous stages of the twenties. With all eight rooms in view and illuminated, Stein could employ one of his favourite techniques: continuing silent action while the dialogue drew the major focus to one point on stage.

The image of a tenement house, opened up to reveal its occupants, isolated but hardly individualized, disturbingly similar in their emptiness yet unable to communicate with one another, this image characterizes Stein's pessimistic though not nihilistic view of the society in which he lives. It was no doubt, in part, this insight which had turned him towards the rich humanity of Shakespeare and to the production of a play that creates a Utopia in the Forest of Arden.

Confrontation with Shakespeare –
Shakespeare's Memory and *As You Like It*

For centuries Shakespeare has occupied a special place in German theatre. In the seventeenth century wandering English players toured Germany with crude versions of *Hamlet* and *Titus Andronicus*, and in the eighteenth century, while France generally dismissed Shakespeare as an untutored barbarian, Lessing hailed him as the source of inspiration for a new national theatre. Shakespeare's influence on German playwriting was considerable: thanks to his example, blank verse replaced alexandrines as the standard metrical form for tragedy, and vigorous realism banished the neo-classical style imitated from the French. Goethe, Schiller, Kleist, Grillparzer, Hebbel and Büchner, in fact, all the major dramatists in the German language up to the end of the nineteenth century, acknowledged their debt to Shakespeare, and Tieck and Schlegel, two leading writers of the Romantic period, devoted a significant part of their careers to rendering his works in German. The Duke of Saxe-Meiningen achieved his greatest successes with Shakespeare productions, and Max Reinhardt's 1905 staging of *A Midsummer Night's Dream*, which used a revolving stage for the first time as an integral element of performance, not only established Reinhardt as a director but also initiated a revolution in the style of German theatre. The most influential productions of the leading expressionist director, Leopold Jessner, were *Richard III* and *Othello* in the early 1920s, and Brecht's first piece of direction was of his own version of an Elizabethan tragedy, Marlowe's *Edward II*. In the nationalist hysteria of the Third Reich there were even attempts to prove that Shakespeare was a German. Today he remains the most frequently performed author on the German stage.

It is small wonder that, even more than in Britain, Shakespeare is felt by the Germans to be *vorbelastet* (weighed down with all that has gone before). Responses to this feeling vary from staging wearily conventional versions of his plays to extraordinarily inventive but often distorted renderings of his work, like Zadek's *Lear* in vaudeville style or Heyme's *Hamlet* performed amongst a vast array of video cameras and monitors, with a bleeding horse suspended at the back of the performing area.

Characteristically for Stein and his ensemble, their approach to

Shakespeare was one of extreme caution. Their concern was not so much to establish how Shakespeare could best make an impact on a modern audience, but rather to rediscover the world which Shakespeare inhabited and so understand the social and cultural forces that shaped his writing. From January 1971 until 1973, under the guidance of Botho Strauss, the ensemble met regularly for seminars on Shakespeare, and already proposals for performing *Othello, Richard II, Troilus and Cressida* or *The Tempest* were considered. Stein joined the Shakespeare group when it was reconvened early in 1975. After spending some time considering the suitability of various texts for performance, the ensemble moved on to an exploration of aspects of Elizabethan culture and society. In the words of Elke Petri (quoted in Lackner, *Drama Review*, T74 (1977), 81):

Then we began studying more about Shakespeare's time and cultural context. Stein, Sturm and the assistant directors compiled a reading list of related literature – other authors of the time, natural science, philosophy, theatre practice. Each actor chose subjects that interested him, and did independent research that he then shared with the others in the weekly staff meetings. Each actor began training in several skills new to him – alone, with private teachers, or in groups. One girl learned the lute, another group studied Gesualdo madrigals – practicing [sic] for more than half a year – circus skills, acrobatics. But we had no set plan, and the more research and training we did, the more we realized the immensity of the task.

Although there was no "set plan," their research could be seen to fall under various headings:

1. Elizabethan theatre
2. Sources of the theatre and related arts
3. Natural sciences and philosophy
4. Political practice and theory
5. Elizabethan patterns of thought

Comprehensive as these researches seemed, there were surprising omissions: there was scant treatment of Elizabethan stagecraft, the use of boy actors, for example, or the physical staging conditions of Shakespeare's own theatres. Then there was little reference beyond the four humours to medicine and hardly any to religion, both of which topics occur significantly in Shakespeare's writings. Indeed, little attention was paid to the ordinary life of a citizen in Elizabeth's England; admittedly, sources for such research may be harder to come by than writings on astronomy, but they would have provided a more vital picture of the age. As it was, the academic bias of the collective's study was to colour Stein's treatment of *As You Like It*. It seems at times that he had forgotten that Shakespeare was as interested in eating food as in watching the stars.

Nevertheless, despite these reservations, one cannot help but admire the seriousness and industry that characterized the ensemble's confrontation with Shakespeare, a period of preparation possibly unequalled in the history of theatre and an undertaking unthinkable in the poorly subsidized theatres of Shakespeare's homeland.

After so much work, both in terms of reading and developing particular skills, it was felt that the Schaubühne should present its findings to the public. The result, a kind of living museum of the Elizabethan age, was given the English title of *Shakespeare's Memory* – the English word containing a double meaning, expressed by the German *Erinnerung* (the thing remembered) and *Gedächtnis* (the faculty of memory). It was presented over two evenings in the CCC Film Studios in Spandau, opening on the 22 and 23 December 1976. Although never purporting to be a theatrical performance as such and despite the fact that the event took place several miles from the centre of Berlin, the "performances" were sold out for months in advance.

The programme of events has been documented in English by Peter Lackner in his article on Peter Stein in *Drama Review*, T74 (1977), 79–102, so a brief summary will here suffice. The first item consisted of various forms of folk entertainment: masked procession, morris dancing, fencing, acrobatics, musical contributions and folk drama (a mummers' play and *The Second Shepherd's Pageant*). The audience of some 360 had remained standing until now, moving around to view the different acts, many of which were performed simultaneously in spaces cleared in their midst by the actors.

For the second item banquet tables were rolled out, and the audience were invited to sit for food and drink, while the show continued in the aisle between the tables. Pageant wagons were pulled in, one at first bearing personifications of grammar, rhetoric and dialectics, and then academicians in debate. Another wagon carried a "cage of fools" who dismounted to perform *The Revesby Play,* a piece of folk drama incorporating a dance with swords. Interspersed with this, speeches were delivered from galleries around the hall, for example, Elizabeth's Tilbury speech before the battle against the Spanish Armada. At the end of this section the tables were cleared, while an extract from a radio production by Kortner of *King Lear* was played – a "tribute to Fritz Kortner."

The final item of the first evening was entitled "The Museum." It was here that the ensemble displayed its erudition about astronomy, using models, instruments and a planetarium. This developed into presentations of astrological theory (Elizabeth's horoscope, zodiac man) and concluded with a visit to the adjacent "Garden of Sympa-

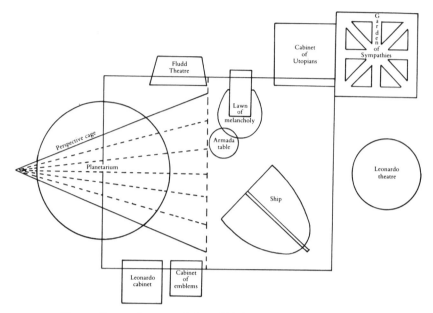

Fig. 9   Composite groundplan of *Shakespeare's Memory*.

thies," where intersecting passages displayed exhibits about the Renaissance conception of humours and correspondences, and to the "Cabinet of Utopians" containing life-size models of various utopian beings: the hermaphrodite, the androgynous man, the hermit, the embryo, the zodiac man and the man of humours.

The second evening opened in "The Museum," recapitulating elements from the previous evening. In place of the planetarium, a "perspective cage" had been erected, a construction of cardboard figures and wires demonstrating theories of perspective in Renaissance art. In a "Cabinet of Emblems" Rüdiger Hacker and Ilse Ritter humorously demonstrated rhetorical gestures. Most of this section, however, was devoted to the theme of melancholy, including an extract from Robert Burton's *Anatomy of Melancholy*, performed by Otto Sander in a circular theatre based on a design by Leonardo da Vinci.

"The Museum" now turned its attention to the figure of Elizabeth. Christine Oesterlein as the aging Elizabeth and Sabine Andreas as the young Queen, both in richly authentic costumes, delivered speeches from raised platforms, litters and pageant wagons. These

20 *Shakespeare's Memory.* "Lawn of Melancholy": "lady in fancy–
dress" (Jutta Lampe) after a painting by Marcus Gheeraerts.

were interspersed with addresses to the Queen and statements about the nature of kingship. At the same time a scene from Tourneur's *The Revenger's Tragedy* was performed.

At the end of this section a huge cross-section of a ship was wheeled in. This provided the setting for accounts of voyages into the New World and of the effects of colonization. Nearby, using model ships, the course of the Battle of the Armada was explained.

The whole event ended with a series of set pieces from Shakespeare's plays, performed on an "island" of tables, wagons and rostra. Although the speeches were grouped loosely according to theme, the programme freely admitted that they were chosen "arbitrarily

21 *Shakespeare's Memory. "Descensus astraeae"*: the young Elizabeth (Sabine Andreas) and her court.

22 *Shakespeare's Memory.* "The Ship": the Armada table is unloaded.

according to our preferences." It was here that one might have expected the preparation to have borne fruit in performance. As it was, the delivery of the speeches was singularly unexciting. There were inventive elements in the presentation: the figure of Time from *The Winter's Tale* hovered over the island in the reconstruction of an Elizabethan flying harness; Banquo's murderers gathered quietly and slipped away into the audience after completing the deed; Titania (Jutta Lampe) addressed her speech to a life-size stuffed donkey, thus emphasizing the tender bestiality inherent in the situation (although hardly a practical proposal for presenting the figure of Bottom in the play). But the quality of acting in these "highlights from Shakespeare" left much to be desired. As Benjamin Hinrichs observed (*Die Zeit*, 31 December 1976):

there might have been satisfactory ways of performing this revue – academically as careful recitation, or in a popular manner with the joyful panache of travelling players. What made a mockery of the idea was the communal attempt in the last of the seven hours to attempt to play Shakespeare properly – it ended in an exhibition of outmoded theatre styles, in Christmas-card schmaltz, repertory theatre emotionalism, and mannered intensity.

It would have been within the resources and intelligence of the Schaubühne ensemble to have attempted a reconstruction of at least a part of a Shakespeare play to bring together some of the ideas they had explored, but there seems to have been an understandable decision to wait for the forthcoming Shakespeare production before presenting anything more than brief extracts.

What had the two evenings of *Shakespeare's Memory* achieved for the ensemble and the public? In terms of presentation, Stein's first attempt at a promenade staging was a breakthrough for the Schaubühne. The randomness of the experience was something which Stein had distrusted for the performance of plays. Asked by Bernard Dort (*Travail théâtral*, 1972, p. 33) whether Stein might not attempt to invite participation by using a promenade staging, he replied:

No, I find that a load of rubbish. It's not my style at all. I don't see in it any means of overcoming distance, nothing but short-lived entertainment. If it's done to entertain, fine, I have nothing against it . . . Don't tell me it's audience participation: the events are shown in a certain way, not in any other, and the audience are powerless to change anything. They are merely given the appearance of freedom by moving towards a noise. That's a way of pushing them around, of constraining them, not of giving them their freedom.

Now, in *Shakespeare's Memory*, the audience were to some extent free to compose their own show. Since many events were performed simultaneously, the spectator could select what he saw, could approach the performers or walk away from them, could even retire to the bar for refreshment and return when it pleased him. In fact, the event was described by some critics as being like a living pro-gramme – the kind of lavishly illustrated material that the ensemble had collected for *Peer Gynt* here brought to life in a theatrical manner.

To be able to respond to the event as though leafing through the pages of a magazine instead of paying the usual rapt and focussed attention expected of a theatre audience was a special experience for the visitor to *Shakespeare's Memory*. The German theatre, more than most, creates a distance between actor and audience. Here all shared the same light, all were free to stand and move, and the spectator could, in the Museum section, even ask the actor to repeat or clarify some of his text. The gulf separating performer from public was decisively bridged.

For the actors, the experience was a valuable one. The Schaubühne company had for some time played in a sensitive, thought-out, dis-ciplined, almost introverted style. Now they were required to move amongst the audience, to address individuals in close proximity, and to vie with each other for the attention of the spectators. Most critics at the première were aware of a certain inhibition in the ensemble. Later this seems to have been overcome, an indication that this was a valuable learning experience for the actors.

In terms of content, the difficulty lay in communicating the enthu-siasm experienced by the ensemble in gathering their information. As Hinrichs said (*Die Zeit,* 31 December 1976), a lion hunt may be exciting, but all that remains is a stuffed head: "The Schaubühne cannot present its explorations to the public but merely its results; not the adventure itself, only a few trophies. The pride with which they are shown is sometimes rather childish, often an intimidating and precocious showing-off ('look, this is how educated you have to be to understand Shakespeare')." The trophies that were on display did however communicate some important ideas to the audience. Because Shakespeare's genius makes his plays so vibrant and still so relevant to our own era, it is easily forgotten how much a man of his own age he was, conditioned by the politics and philosophy of the Elizabethan age. For one thing, his plays were not composed as time-less literary products but as popular art forms, incorporating and exploiting many of the folk elements of his culture. Thus, there was a point in the ensemble presenting folk plays, dances and acrobatic feats. Unfortunately, the intelligent and subtle style of the Schau-bühne actors was at odds with the crude fairground techniques needed for these virtuoso displays – "Shakespeare in underpants," a phrase Stein once coined with reference to Zadek's work. As Hell-muth Karasek observed in *Der Spiegel* (3 January 1977, p. 78): "Their determination to be folk-performers reminded one of students from a Jesuit seminary playing football with tramps and down-and-outs. It was sentimentally patronizing."

In addition to tracing Shakespeare's debt to the popular artistic traditions of his age, the major thrust of the Schaubühne's explora-tion, and its greatest contribution to an understanding of Shake-speare, was concerned with the science and superstition of the Re-naissance. Philosophers had abandoned the orthodoxy of the medieval church but had only begun to evolve the empirical method; astronomers were gaining new insights into the structure of the uni-verse, while complete credence was still lent to astrological predic-tions; Queen Elizabeth was the head of a politically complex, modern state and yet still surrounded with the aura of the divine right of kingship. Suspended between the superstitions of the Middle Ages and the impending rationalism of Western Europe, the Elizabethan age contained within it a mass of fruitful contradictions, and its greatest playwright embraced these totally. Thus it is that Shake-speare seems at once so relevant and accessible and at the same time so mysterious and metaphysical. Like Hamlet, he reasons with the acuteness of a Wittenberg student yet sees clearly the ghosts of the past.

With customary modesty Stein admitted (*Die Zeit,* 31 December 1976): "We approached Shakespeare as we would a great continent, and perhaps our navigational means were not quite adequate; maybe the boats were too small and the sails too big." Whether the ensemble made a landing or merely studied the maps remained to be seen when the long awaited Shakespeare production took place.

There was naturally considerable discussion about what text to perform. For some time it seemed as though it would be *Richard II* with Otto Sander, who had presented the prison monologue in "Shakespeare's Island," in the title-role. Eventually, however, after, for example, rejecting *Twelfth Night* as being "too obvious," the choice fell on *As You Like It.*

The advantages of this piece were many: it treated several of the themes explored by the ensemble – the good and bad ruler, the androgynous figure of Rosalind/Ganymede, and folk elements of pas-toral life. This last theme, the escape to the Forest of Arden, was particularly relevant to a West Berlin audience. Some woodland, crowded at weekends, lies within the boundaries of West Berlin, but it is impossible – short of travelling for hours across the territory of the German Democratic Republic to the West German border – to escape from this urban enclave to wide expanses of countryside. It was understandable and appropriate, therefore, that Stein's production should be so strongly aware of the theme of escaping to a pastoral Utopia – and aware too of the precarious nature of this escape.

In the first discussions of the Shakespeare group which Stein attended, he expressed his dissatisfaction with most Shakespearean productions. These had emphasized "the historical aspect, which had least interested and moved him" (Protocol no. 444, 2 January 1975) – a surprising admission from someone who spent so long penetrating the historical context of any piece he directs. It would seem, however, that Stein's quarrel was with the quality of historical pageant which so often encumbers Shakespeare, depriving his plays of freshness. Instead, Stein argued, "we must use as our starting-point the forest, which has 'magical qualities' and which is both wild and pleasant . . . In the scenes in which affairs of state are referred to, we will to some extent adopt the idiom of the history plays" (Protocol no. 450, 22 January 1975). On the same occasion Stein admitted that this play seemed "totally foreign" to him, "so full of ideas, so complex and so lacking in consistency that he for one found it hard to come to terms with."

By all accounts the rehearsal period was not a happy one. Overwhelmed by the vastness of Shakespeare's genius, Stein at times seemed to lose his nerve. He did not provide the calm leadership the ensemble had come to expect of him, and things worsened when he fell from a catwalk and broke his arm. He discharged himself from hospital against the advice of the doctors and suffered recurrent headaches from the accident. The confident clarity which had consistently characterized his work now appeared almost impossible to achieve. Unlike Zadek, who blithely launches himself into Shakespeare, allowing conceptions to develop through improvisation with his ensemble, Peter Stein, after years of patient research now seemed intimidated by the complexity of the material. This crisis of self-confidence created within the cast the kind of tensions common to many theatres but mercifully rare at the Schaubühne. It is unfair, however, to dwell on these preparatory difficulties: in discussing a painting it is seldom relevant to be concerned with the agonies the artist passed through while working on it or with how short-tempered he became towards his wife. It is relevant, though, to suggest that the very thorough research of the ensemble inhibited a spontaneous approach to Shakespeare. After all, he himself wrote and performed his plays for quick commercial gain. Stein was aware of the danger of "bookishness": when at an early meeting Günter Lampe read from Jung's *Mysterium coniunctionis* to illustrate utopian love in the symbol of the hermaphrodite, Stein warned against an over-use of secondary literature and insisted on the need to retain a certain "impulsiveness" (Protocol no. 450, 22 January 1975).

Whatever the roads that led there, Stein's production of *As You Like It* (*Wie es euch gefällt*), which opened on 20 September 1977, was to be the most spectacular presentation of Shakespeare in Germany since Reinhardt and arguably the most significant Shakespeare production since Peter Brook's *A Midsummer Night's Dream*. It took place in the CCC Film Studios where *Shakespeare's Memory* had been performed nine months previously. Once again Stein felt it necessary to abandon the constraints of the Schaubühne am Halleschen Ufer, despite the fact that this added considerably to the cost of the production, involved cast and technicians in hours of travel each week and obliged Berlin audiences to go to almost unprecedented lengths to reach the "theatre."

On arrival the audience were herded by way of a temporary wooden box office into a long, high hall, where they remained standing for the first part of the play. The walls and ceiling were of a pale powder-blue, illuminated from spots set below grills in raised walks and platforms on three sides of the hall. The pale-blue tone and concealed lighting produced an unreal, cold effect, rather as though one were standing inside a glacier. On the platforms at the perimeter sat the actors and actresses, so immobile (with the exception of Rosalind who wept silently) that they seemed like waxworks. The costumes, designed by Moidele Bickel, were authentically Elizabethan, elaborate affairs encrusted with pearls and fretted with gold and silver, but, except for Touchstone's motley, muted in colour – blacks, chocolate-browns and greys.

Once the audience were assembled, the play began. The scenes near Oliver's house and in Frederick's court, that is, the first act and Act II, scenes ii and iii, and Act III, scene i, were cross-cut in a cinematic style of juxtaposition, "a tableau of widely different impulses," as Stein described it (Protocol no. 450, 22 January 1975). One actor or group would speak a few lines and freeze into a tableau while a passage from another scene was interposed from other players elsewhere in the hall. In place of the leisurely exposition of Shakespeare's play, therefore, one had the exciting rhythms of montage, or as David Zane Mairowitz put it (*Plays and Players*, vol. 25, no. 3 (1977) 18): this "has the effect . . . of interweaving the various plots and character fates so that their dilemmas are witnessed in immediate confrontation rather than in reflection."

The physical use of this area was interesting and doubtless a result of the ensemble's researches into Elizabethan theatre, in particular the Great Hall performances. The audience standing at the feet of the actors and free to move towards the focus of attention shared something of the experience of the Elizabethan groundlings – an informal relationship between actor and audience, which Touchstone was particularly able to exploit, directing many of his asides to spectators a few feet away from him.

This proximity was increased when two lords appeared and, exchanging the information ascribed to Charles and Oliver in the original (i,i), moved amongst the audience like two nobles conversing in a busy London street. Because "overheard," the lines made a much greater impact than is normally the case when actors, framed by a proscenium arch, try to impart information in a natural manner.

The most exciting and authentic moment was on the entry of Charles to the wrestling-match. He was preceded by a lord who called out: "Make way! Make way for Charles, the Duke's wrestler!" and so created a path through the middle of the audience. The exploration of Elizabethan staging methods in the *Shakespeare's Memory* programme had produced interesting possibilities for this production.

The wrestling-match itself was the showpiece of this first part, and for it Stein had engaged a professional wrestler. As a result Charles's lines had to be re-allocated, and most of them were spoken by Le Beau, referring to Charles in the third person. Orlando, played by the strikingly beautiful Michael König stripped to a loin-cloth, matched himself against this forbidding heavyweight. After a sequence of carefully rehearsed holds and throws, Orlando found himself almost to his own surprise lifting Charles upside-down off the ground to dash him to unconsciousness at the Duke's feet. The whole thing was so polished and the moves so premeditated that it failed to convince as a spontaneous conflict. In retrospect, however, this was no doubt precisely what Stein intended; for later, as we shall see, Orlando wrestled for his very life with a wild beast. This early contest was not allowed to develop too much tension; it was a public display of strength, whereas the later fight was to the death.

The wrestling-match characterized the whole level of performance of this first part. The acting was neither strongly stylized nor did it possess the naturalness and spontaneity of good realistic acting.

Oliver (Eberhard Feik) was a melodramatic villain, Adam (Gerd David), bent double and falsetto-voiced, presented an actor's stereotype of senility. The performances had in general something of that irritatingly stilted manner which is characteristic of so many German municipal theatres.

The relief from such solemnity that might have been expected from Touchstone was hardly forthcoming either. The Shakespearean clown is a problematic figure for a modern audience: he all too often seems a curious appendage, and his jokes seldom strike us as funny. So we have recourse time and again to the melancholy fool, a weary character whose wit is dulled, whose laughter is hollow. Here too

23 *As You Like It.* Orlando (Michael König) defeats Charles in the cold white setting of Frederick's court (I, ii).

Werner Rehm played Touchstone as a pathetic, fleshy, and infantile clown: his voice squeaked, he sucked his thumb, he adopted sulky attitudes. Occasionally he was disturbingly grotesque, as when he entertained Rosalind and Celia by producing a dead mouse from his mouth.

Only Jutta Lampe as Rosalind discovered cross-currents in her playing. Consumed with grief over her father, she could still giggle with Celia (Tina Engel) and both touch and amuse us with her sudden love for Orlando. After giving her chain to Orlando, she shyly ran away behind a pillar, peered round, then asked: "Did you call, sir?" And before the love-struck Orlando could reply, she leapt down the steps to him to confess: "Sir, you have wrestled well, and over-thrown/More than your enemies." Such spontaneity broke through the stiff formality of the court and was a clue that the stilted playing proceeded from a deliberate and brave directorial decision. The slow pacing of the lines, the rhetorical gestures, the pedantic delivery of "Stage German," the rather unsubtle characterization, all these were means to make the court scenes of the play uncomfortable and oppressive. The only adequate and sensitive response was to seek to escape from this cold, blue-white world, in which dark-clad actors from above bore down heavily on the audience. Stein risked the dissatisfaction of the audience (and I for one was misled into sensing disappointment at the woodenness of the acting) in order to prepare for the entry into the Forest of Arden. Here we did not merely observe characters moving into the green innocence of Nature; we experienced the release ourselves.

This was achieved as follows: the first part ended with Frederick issuing orders to Oliver to pursue Orlando into the Forest of Arden (iii,i). Over loudspeakers the barking of hounds resounded around the hall, and Oliver and his servants exited by a door in one of the walls. The audience were invited to follow, and left the hall in single file, each one like Alice at the door into Wonderland garden.

We found ourselves in a dimly lit, green labyrinth, artificial creepers hanging from above, water dripping down the walls. As we followed the twists and turns of this passage, we passed curious collages pasted on the walls, small booth-like openings containing, for example, an Elizabethan workshop or, more strikingly, the androgynous man from *Shakespeare's Memory*, a life-size plaster statue with fully formed breasts and a penis bulging from his/her breeches. As the sound of the barking dogs grew distant, we began to hear the hunting-horns of Arden beckoning us forwards. The conception was brilliant: to pass from the formality and brutality of the court through an underground labyrinth to the freedom and innocence of the forest was like being born anew – a metaphorical journey through the uterine canal. The exhibits on the way often seemed arbitrary and self-consciously clever, however. As Henning Rischbieter wondered (*Theater heute*, 1977/11, p. 11): "Is this not already the point in this production where what is superfluous begins to take over from what is necessary?"

The almost random fullness of image and activity became even more apparent as the audience entered Karl-Ernst Herrmann's magnificent set for the Forest of Arden. A complete woodland environment had been created in the vast film studios. The air was filled with the sound of bird-song and music, golden light fell from above, some of it through the leaves of a fine beech tree, which had been transplanted from woodland on the outskirts of Berlin. Beneath the beech was a shallow pool of water bounded at one side by a field of corn. This sylvan scene formed a kind of backdrop for the main acting area, which measured some forty feet by one hundred feet and

Fig. 10 *As You Like It*. The Forest of Arden.

which was surrounded by a horseshoe arrangement of about three hundred seats. There were more acting areas on catwalks around the walls of the studio, in the aisles between the seats and on raised levels amongst and above the audience – Audrey's home, the farmstead which Rosalind purchases, and so on. The woodland setting was further achieved by suspending tree trunks around the studio and filling empty areas with foliage, greensward, and articles of rural life – a loom, a butter-churn, a rowing-boat – and collections made by the nobles in exile – cases of stuffed birds, insects and fossils. More arbitrary were some remnants from *Shakespeare's Memory*, as, for example, a huge model of the Ptolemaic universe suspended from the ceiling of the studio. In addition, an electric organ was mounted in a pillar to one side of the acting area.

As the audience were directed to their seats where they were to remain without break for the rest of the play, they became aware of figures in this forest setting, engaged in activities appropriate to their station: lords ordering their ornithological or entomological collections, Audrey churning butter, a hunter firing a live round into the tree causing a shower of leaves, and so on. The abundant variety of activity continued simultaneously with the spoken scenes, so providing a continuing environmental experience. Apart from a total concentration during some of the more important scenes, there was nearly always something for the eye to catch. As with *Summerfolk* it was impossible to see everything at one performance: throughout the evening a witch-like figure (Christine Oesterlein) kept appearing briefly, a hermit covered only with long hair would rush along a catwalk muttering to himself, a straw man wandered in and out, Robin Hood put in an appearance, as did Robinson Crusoe sporting a goatskin umbrella and shouting for Man Friday. The Forest of Arden became a wonderland of busy rusticity and exotic creatures. As David Zane Mairowitz commented (*Plays and Players*, vol. 25, no. 3 (1977) 18): "In this manner, the concept of 'scene change' is abandoned and the play simply travels visually from tension to tension or from tension to relief, without significant pause." Indeed, Stein had initially considered the possibility of allowing the audience, in the promenade style of *Shakespeare's Memory*, to wander freely through the "forest," but it would have been difficult to achieve the necessary focus. As it was, the audience remained stationary, while the action moved from level to level and from area to area.

It began high up beside one section of the audience. The courtiers of the exiled Duke (Günter Lampe) shiveringly drew a tarpaulin closer round their master as he attempted to persuade them that "sweet are the uses of adversity" (ii, i), a convincing way of handling the speech and a reminder that Arden too had its very real drawbacks. During this, Jaques (Peter Fitz) could already be seen wandering around in his role of observer, a function he maintained almost unceasingly throughout the performance. Glowering in the background in travelling-coat with tartan shawl, he gave the impression of an irascible Scot.

Moidele Bickel's costumes in this part of the play were totally different from the authentic dress of the court scenes. With a vague suggestion of the late nineteenth century, for example, in the elegant beige suit and wide-brimmed hat later worn by Orlando, the costumes lifted the Forest of Arden out of the historical setting of the court into a virtually timeless situation.

So when Rosalind entered with Celia and Touchstone (ii, iv), it came as no great surprise to see her with a fur cap and jerkin, and Touchstone pulling a cart laden with seven suitcases. They began their scene quite close to the actor playing Corin (Otto Mächtlinger) who, however, ignored their presence. Thus the use of the Elizabethan convention was established that actors may be physically close on stage but only seem to become aware of one another when the scene required it. Initially, this was a surprise, but in fact it is no more odd than the convention that allows the presence of the audience to be ignored until an aside is addressed to it.

Some of the folk elements which the ensemble had explored for *Shakespeare's Memory* could now be recalled here. As the exiled lords sat down to a meal (ii, vii), they protected themselves with a circle of brushwood, a practical device to deter snakes but also a magical encircling, like the circle that Jaques drew round the lords on his "ducdame" song. When Jaques then related his encounter with the fool in the forest (commented on in witty asides by Touchstone, sprawling in the rowing-boat) and declared: "I am ambitious for a motley coat," the lords obliged by covering him with ribbons and giving him a crown of leaves – an authentic image of the Lord of Misrule.

Orlando burst in upon this merry gathering, his sword drawn in a display of youthful bravado, bringing with him the violence of the court. The Duke and his followers unflinchingly calmed his aggression and Amiens soothed him with music in characteristically Elizabethan fashion. When Jaques prepared to deliver his "Seven Ages of Man" speech, Stein indicated that this was no spontaneous philosophizing by Jaques but the recitation of a familiar piece of folk wisdom. Encouraged by the lords to perform his "party piece," Jaques moved to a raised piece of greensward and, striking a series of rhetorical poses, delivered the speech in its English original, to the delighted applause of the Duke's entourage. With the Duke's welcome to Orlando this section of the play ended: Rosalind and Orlando were both established now in the Forest of Arden, and the ground was prepared for their first meeting.

This took the form of a peaceful interlude – a bucolic idyll after the movement, humour and loudness of the second act, as though Nature were quietly gathering its strength to move forward into the summer scenes of Act III. The lighting grew warmer, organ music (composed by Peter Michael Hamel) quietly played, Phebe (Elke

24 *As You Like It.* Touchstone (Werner Rehm), Celia (Tina Engel) and Rosalind (Jutta Lampe) arrive in the Forest of Arden (II, iv).

Petri) sauntered to the pool and began, Narcissus-like, to admire her own reflection, Corin unpacked bags of stones, sods, herbs and flowers into piles on the central acting area, and Orlando wandered amongst the trees, hanging up sheaves of love-poems to Rosalind while devising compounds beginning with "Ros–": "rose-red," "rose-tree," and so on. As he reached Corin's piles in the acting area, he began to arrange each pile to spell out the letters of Rosalind's name. Meanwhile, Touchstone and Corin discussed the "shepherd's life" on a platform in front of Rosalind's homestead.

Rosalind was dressed in a loose-fitting shirt and white cotton trousers which reached to her calves, with a floppy hat on her head and a moustache painted on her upper lip – more an urchin than the pretty boy common to productions of *As You Like It*. The more strongly built Tina Engel as Celia wore a "sailor-suit" dress and carried a butterfly-net – all youth and sunshine, reminding of Edwardian summers. Between the two actresses there was an extraordinary intimacy of communication, all the more remarkable because at times during rehearsals this had seemed almost impossible to achieve.

Particularly memorable was the delighted mockery of Celia as she adorned Rosalind with sheet after sheet of love-poems or laughed with unconcealed delight before the line: "Change you colour?" When Orlando and Rosalind then met and he agreed to her plan to personate his sweetheart, Celia stood at a distance throwing clods of earth at Rosalind – a typical Stein device of anticipating a later line with appropriate action. In Act IV, scene i, Celia mockingly expresses her indignation: "You have simply misus'd our sex in your love-prate." By slinging mud at Rosalind she had already shown her disapproval in an amusingly theatrical way.

Despite the natural and relaxed style of these encounters, Stein did not attempt to force psychological naturalism on them. On 22 January 1975, he had already said of Rosalind (Protocol no. 450): "it is impossible to approach these events in a psychological manner, because they cannot be played that way." They would have to find "something more theatrical, treat it like some kind of a sport (e.g. a boxing-match). Each member of the audience will anyway at any given point introduce psychological dimensions for himself." The reference to boxing suggests one progenitor of this acting style: Brecht. While not specifically "Brechtian," the acting style Stein devised for the forest scenes certainly possessed Brechtian elements: a beguiling informality, a cheekily irreverent tone and the emphasis on situation rather than on individual psychology.

25 *As You Like It.* Phebe (Elke Petri) by the pool.

This inventively fresh approach to Shakespeare's text was apparent in the next scene (III, iii), in which Touchstone attempted to marry Audrey with the assistance of the rustic vicar, Sir Oliver Martext. Conventionally, Martext is played as a clerical buffoon. Here, presented by Otto Sander, he possessed a quiet dignity and an unruffled serenity despite his bizarre accoutrements. Opening a minuscule suitcase, he produced from it a collapsible table, a collapsible chalice and a stole which he solemnly kissed before laying it over his shoulders. When he discovered that there was no one "to give the woman," he silently and seriously folded his stole after kissing it, collapsed the chalice and the table and packed them into his case. When Jaques came forward to give Audrey away, everything was unpacked once more, only to be returned when Jaques took Touchstone off to be married in a church.

Silvius's declaration of love for Phebe, the "pageant truly play'd," was performed by the actors, Wolf Redl and Elke Petri, on a stage especially erected over the pool. In this way the scene was given a theatrical context and delivered as an eclogue. While this pointed to the literary sources of Shakespeare's dialogue, and provided a strong moment when Rosalind sharply intervened to upbraid Phebe for her pride, it lifted the scene from the portrayal of a genuine emotional relationship to a staged display of feeling, a piece of sophistication at odds with Phebe's simple-minded arrogance and Silvius's dog-like devotion.

By contrast, the mock-wedding between Orlando and Rosalind/Ganymede was performed like a children's game, with Celia assuming a priest-like voice and striking the couple with her butterfly-net to prompt them. The disadvantage in rendering the relationship between Orlando and his substitute beloved so innocent, childlike and flirtatious, was that the dangers of the situation never became apparent. What if Orlando came to love the pretty boy more than his absent sweetheart? How much was his love already a homosexual passion? "There was no trace of these perilous depths in the relationship of the main characters," commented Benjamin Hinrichs (*Die Zeit*, 30 September 1977).

Once more eschewing psychological subtleties, Stein externalized this androgynous nexus in the most effective and disturbing part of the play. The short scene (IV, ii), in which a slain deer is brought in, included the actual skinning of the deer and the draping of the hide over one of the lords. The other lords with horns on their heads danced a primitive hunting dance. The lights dimmed eerily and Rosalind and Celia fell asleep in each other's arms. Orlando could be observed painting his face like a woman (cf. König painting himself like a clown in *Summerfolk*) and caressing his breasts. The figure draped with the deerskin then confronted Orlando and they became locked in violent struggle, while Rosalind and Celia rolled across the ground in a tight embrace. Understandably, Stein refuses to "explain" this episode: "Orlando's fight was not one of the most thought-out aspects of my *As You Like It* production. It formed a part of a dreamlike mime sequence which possessed musical and visual meaning rather than any narrow interpretable significance" (personal communication, 18 October 1980).

A rational interpretation would not exhaust the implications of this episode, but it is clear that the erotic implications of Shake-

26 *As You Like It.* Orlando (Michael König) paints his face while the lords dance a primitive hunting dance (IV, ii).

speare's play, which Jan Kott discusses in his "Bitter Arcadia" essay, reprinted in the Schaubühne programme, were here explored. Rosalind, originally played by a boy actor, pretends to be a boy, Ganymede, who for Orlando's sake pretends to be Rosalind. This blurring of sexual difference is more than an excuse for an intriguing plot: it represents the ancient search for a love which transcends the division between male and female, not the love of man for woman or woman for man but a total union of loving in which, to use Jungian terms, *animus* and *anima* are at one. So, while Rosalind and Celia experienced the sexual embrace of two women, Orlando struggled with a wild, horned beast, emblematic of his violent masculine nature. Exhausted but victorious, he was now able to be truly worthy of Rosalind's love.

The life-and-death struggle of Orlando with the wild beast adumbrated his reported fight with the lioness to save his brother, Oliver. After Oliver had related Orlando's fight to Rosalind and Celia, he produced the "napkin/ Dy'd in his blood." Instead of the usual red-stained cloth, he held up a piece of clean white linen with a small red spot in its centre. At the sight of it Rosalind fainted away. Once again strict psychological plausibility was sacrificed for theatrical surprise and wit, and a moment of psychological truth for the truth of the comic situation – that Rosalind's intense love ultimately removes all disguise: "This was not counterfeit; there is too great testimony in your complexion that it was a passion of earnest." Curiously, and seemingly contrary to Shakespeare's intentions, Celia and Oliver fell into each other's arms over Rosalind's swooning body, embracing with all the familiarity of lovers of long standing. Perhaps this "giddiness," this "sudden wooing" was intended to provide a contrast, as indeed it does in Shakespeare, with the lengthy game of paying court to Rosalind. In a personal communication (18 October 1980) Stein challenged the accepted view of Celia and Oliver's courtship, which I adopt above: "How do you know how quickly Oliver and Celia fall in love or what Shakespeare intended? His play is full of even more incredible incidents."

At last the plot complications could be resolved. Rosalind promised a solution to the yearnings of Orlando, Silvius and Phebe in the formal declarations of love in Act v, scene ii. Reflecting the liturgical character of this hymn to love with its antiphonal responses, Stein placed the four actors in exact symmetry in a circle so that the expressions of love passed from one to another with Rosalind's "And I for no woman" delivered to the world at large. Act v, scene iv followed immediately with Rosalind reaffirming her promises to the Duke.

At this point there was a crashing and tearing, and some dozen knights in armour burst through the tall door at the opposite end from the pond. Again, Stein had taken a reported incident, Duke Frederick's intended invasion of Arden, and acted it out. As the warriors hacked their way through the forest, they began to grow weary, as though overpowered by some magic power of the forest. They cast off their armour piece by piece and collapsed onto the ground or into the pond. Yet again the utopian spirit of Arden had repelled this violent onslaught launched from the court.

Now the wedding wagon rolled in, with Hymen (Gerd David) standing aloft, a gilt figure in an ornate tunic and skirt surrounded by gilt branches. This apparition of Elizabethan kitsch was a warning of the return to artificiality that was to befall the Duke, his followers and the newly wed couples. Already Celia and Rosalind stood resplendent in their court clothes, and they were joined by Orlando and Oliver, once more wearing the dress of Elizabethan noblemen. Dressed less stylishly, but with a sense of occasion, were Touchstone and Audrey and Silvius and Phebe. The last, miserable to discover Ganymede's true identity, howled throughout the ensuing courtly minuet. Civilization had come to Arden, and Jaques moved amongst the dancers, giving his final blessings before going to join the Duke in his "religious life."

The wagon began to roll off and all on it called for Jaques to come with them: "Stay, Jaques, stay," but he bowed his way out, determined to enjoy his melancholy solitariness. As Jan Kott astutely observed: "At the end of the play everyone will leave the Forest of Arden; except Jaques. He is the only one who has no reason to leave the forest because he has never believed in it, has never entered Arcadia." (*Shakespeare our contemporary*, p. 231; reprinted in the Schaubühne programme, p. 40).

The Forest of Arden was a temporary respite from the violence of political life, a glimpse of a world where ideal love might be attained, but it could only be an illusion. Kott again: "Shakespeare has no illusions, not even the illusion that one can live without illusions. He takes us into the Forest of Arden in order to show that one must try to escape, although there is no escape; that the Forest of Arden does not exist, but those who do not run away will be murdered." (*ibid.*, pp. 226–7; reprinted in programme, p. 38).

The, by now slowly and silently dancing, couples approached the far end of the forest area, about to enter the same cold, white hall from which they had originally made their escape. Just as the wagon reached the doorway, there was a jolt, and the courtiers hurtled off towards their icy world once more.

Meanwhile, in Arden, Corin began the laborious task of clearing

27 *As You Like It*. To the couples assembled on Hymen's wedding wagon Jaques de Bois (Willem Menne) announces Frederick's conversion (v, iv).

up the mess left by civilization, the abandoned weapons, armour and clothing, somewhat in the same way that Stein began *Summerfolk* with the peasants clearing the mess in the grounds of the *datsha*.

In place of Shakespeare's epilogue one became aware of Frederick, who had also discarded his armour and was now lying at the foot of the beech proclaiming the "The cycle of the seasons," a prose poem by the French writer Francis Ponge, which reads in part (*Le Parti pris des choses*, Paris, 1942, pp. 25–6):

Weary of turning in on themselves during the winter, the trees suddenly take it into their heads that they have been duped. They can no longer endure it: they pour forth their words, a wave, a vomiting of green. They would like to explode into branchfuls of words. So much the worse! That can be arranged somehow! But in fact everything is arranged in advance! There is no freedom in the growth of leaves . . . Always the same leaf, the same manner of unfolding and the same constraints, always leaves that are symmetrical in themselves and symmetrically placed on the tree. Try another leaf! – Still the same! Another! Still the same! Nothing, in short, would stop them except the following observation: "You cannot escape from trees by tree-like means." A renewed weariness, a renewed spiritual inward-turning. "Let all this turn yellow and fall. Let the period of silence approach, the stripping bare, the AUTUMN."

In this piece Stein summarized his view of Arden: the freedom of nature is an illusion. Nature is bound by its own inflexible laws. So while it is valuable and important to glimpse Utopia and to experience it for an evening, the way forward is through restructuring what we have, not through escaping to what we may never have. How this restructuring is to occur, it was not Stein's intention to discuss in this play. He presented us with a vision not a political programme.

That this vision did not possess Stein's accustomed clarity was a source of dismay to many critics, who felt – as Stein seems at times to have done too – that Shakespeare had gobbled him up. On the contrary, it would be fairer to say that Stein had had the courage to work with images he perhaps could not fathom totally himself. Unnerved as he may have been by the experience, it was an essential stage in his maturing as a director and an indication that *As You Like It*, while standing at the end of a period in Stein's development, also represented the beginning of a new creativity.

8   Conclusion – Stein the explorer and the Schaubühne as model

I am . . . inclined to switch subjects, to change in order to attain different modes of work, approaches and results. For this reason our program continually sways back and forth from different positions, which one can see when one looks at everything we've done. But, if someone were to say to me, you have a personal style which you impose upon everyone, force upon them, then I'd say that would be a shame. I don't have this feeling.

(Stein, interview with Zipes, Theater, vol. 9, no. 1 (1977), p. 53.)

It is hard to generalize about the dozen or so years of Stein's work as a director, either in terms of the plays he has produced or the styles he has employed. The range of his productions has been impressive: an improvisational performance on Greek theatre; a Greek trilogy; a theatrical introduction to the age of Shakespeare; a Shakespeare comedy; a Jacobean tragedy; three German classics, one from the "Storm and Stress," one from the classical, and one from the Romantic periods; a French farce; a Norwegian spectacular classic; a Russian realist piece; a Russian revolutionary piece; an Irish comedy; an early Brecht; a Brecht *Lehrstück*; a *Volksstück*; an agitprop documentary; the West German and the German-language premières of two Bond pieces, one realistic, one fantastical; a contemporary political piece; a Handke; and two plays by Botho Strauss, one of them a world première.

Perhaps the most remarkable aspect of the twenty-three productions for which Stein has been wholly or primarily responsible is that, for all their range, they have been fairly safe choices. Some revivals, like *The Changeling* or *Optimistic Tragedy*, were surprising discoveries, but ones that had already been made, in Britain and East Germany respectively. Stein's production of Handke's *They Are Dying Out* was the sixth on German-language stages, his *Trilogy of Return* was the third. Admittedly, *Great and Small* was a world première, but by now Botho Strauss was an established playwright and little risk was involved.

Stein's brilliance and the resources of the Schaubühne are such that they could afford to follow a much more adventurous policy in their choice of plays. They could, for example, turn an unknown writer into a major celebrity literally overnight, if they chose to. Stein

150

resists such possibilities, however. He insists that he must work with a text of real quality: "There are directors who will take an inferior text and say, 'I'll make this good.' I can't work like that. Unless I know that a text will stand up to critical analysis in rehearsal, I won't use it" (personal communication, 7 December 1977). Furthermore, the democratic processes of decision-making at the Schaubühne take time. Stein had decided he would like to direct *Trilogy of Return* in June 1976, but, given the limited number of productions at the Schaubühne, was only able to realize his intentions in March 1978. By then, understandably, Botho Strauss had agreed to let it be premièred elsewhere, since municipal theatres are always searching for new material of quality. The Schaubühne, by contrast, has no ambitions to get in first with an author or a play: "If someone offers a piece of toilet-paper with the newest hit on it, we couldn't just rush it into performance" (*ibid.*). Besides, Stein points out that the rewriting of classical texts, as in the case of Gorky's *Summerfolk,* resulted in virtually new plays.

For many critics the greatest disappointment in viewing the development of Stein's work is that after *Optimistic Tragedy* in spring 1972 he has directed no overtly political theatre at all. Apart from brief scenes in *Summerfolk* and *Great and Small,* no proletarian has walked across Stein's stage since. The disappointment of his critics stems from the fear that Stein has betrayed his early socialist ideas and is now exclusively involved in aesthetic onanism (*As You Like It*) or the portrayal of bourgeois neuroses (Botho Strauss).

Theatre in the capitalist state is one of the many ways in which the bourgeoisie can preserve their hegemony. It is also a means by which that hegemony can be challenged. There are in West Germany the municipal theatres whose primary function is to reinforce bourgeois consciousness, often by the subtle method of appearing to question social assumptions, when in fact it is individual attitudes that are being challenged and not the fundamental structures of society itself. At the other extreme there is a handful of fringe groups who consistently and from a position of relative independence attempt to raise the consciousness of the proletariat. The problem here is that in the progressive capitalism of the West the exploited classes have lost their sense of identity. They now have very much more than their chains to lose and are consequently resistant to calls for a proletarian revolution. In such a context revolutionary theatre generally operates in a vacuum, only partly filled by left-wing intellectual devotees of a largely bourgeois background. Stein said in 1972 (*Performance* 4 (1972), 70):

If we want to play for workers, then we have to be clear about the fact that the way things stand now, the theater is not being used as an immediate instrument of struggle, and anyway consciousness and social conflict are extremely undeveloped here. So art is hardly needed as an immediate weapon, as agitation; other media do it much better. If we want to play for the people we must find how this theater, as it now exists, can be used. But the working class in itself is not ready or willing or even interested in having a theater, and doesn't need one; while the middle class thinks it *must* have a theater. Thus my primary point of departure is existential survival; one works for and with the bourgeois audience. One must take pains, difficult as it is, to discover, select, and build a theater which will develop those sections of the bourgeois audience which are open.

And in 1973 he is recorded as saying that rather than "adopt a cynical relationship towards the audiences that actually come" to the Schaubühne, the ensemble addresses itself to those "people who do not feel completely happy in their class situation, people who know, have recognized and sense that they must reflect on their class situation if they wish to arrive at ideas that will take them further" (*Kürbiskern* 2 (1973), 336).

Stein might have attempted to reject any compromise with the establishment, an impossibility in the structure of the modern state. He might have remained in obscurity, producing a purist political theatre for those who did not want it. Instead, like Piscator and Brecht before him, he has entered into a degree of compromise with the system; like his left-wing student critics who receive grants from the state, he has to function within the contradictions of capitalism: "All who work here at the Schaubühne – even if they believe that capitalism should be changed or destroyed – stand as individuals within the contradictions of the capitalist system. We carry them with us and we are a part of them. I therefore see no problem in accepting subsidies from the Senate" (*BZ*, 18 January 1971). Once having accepted that he was "forced to make massive compromises" (*Konkret*, 28 January 1971), there seemed no particular virtue in being modest in his claims for subsidies. There is something of a puritanical streak in some left-wing groups who seem to view poor theatre as necessarily being more valid than costly productions. This is indeed the case where lavish stage sets and costumes are a symptom of cynical commercialism. But a revolutionary ideology can employ such means without compromising its integrity. In fact, quite objectively, a political theatre that is well subsidized is freer to pursue its activities than one that is struggling for financial survival. As Stein said to Bernard Dort (*Travail théâtral*, 1972, p. 35):

I don't see why we should work more cheaply when we have the money to do things expensively. Why we should reduce the number of those who

Table 1. *The cost of Stein's productions 1972–8*

	Set	Costumes	Properties	Make-up and wigs
Fegefeuer in Ingolstadt (1972)	30,000 DM	6,000 DM	2,000 DM	350 DM
Das Sparschwein (1973)	170,000 DM	28,000 DM	19,000 DM	12,000 DM
Sommergäste (1974)	37,000 DM	7,000 DM	9,000 DM	5,500 DM
Shakespeare's Memory (1976)	300,000 DM	71,000 DM	26,000 DM	3,500 DM
As You Like It (1977)	242,000 DM	53,500 DM	13,000 DM	2,700 DM
Trilogie des Wiedersehens (1978)	110,000 DM	13,700 DM	2,800 DM	1,000 DM

Approximate sterling equivalents: 1972 – £1 = 8 DM; 1974 – £1 = 6 DM; 1977 – £1 = 4 DM.

work with us, just to be cheap . . . I don't understand why, doing what we do, we are supposed to be more integrated into the capitalist system than the Living Theatre or Grotowski when he performs at one festival after another, admits sixty-nine smart Alecs to his shows – smart Alecs who know nothing about the theatre but who can afford the tickets – and asks the police to drive away all the others . . . Merely to say: "Expensive and lavish materials prevent you from arriving at the truth," that just makes me laugh.

Of course there are risks involved in being an accepted and successful element in the entertainment of the middle classes. As Stein said in 1974 (quoted in Lackner, *Drama Review*, T74 (1977), 102):

As for the accusation from leftists that we are merely a showpiece, a banner for West Germany or Berlin, this is a fact about which we must simply remain clear headed. What should we do to avoid this position – decrease the quality of our work? We must simply see through the negative connotations of this situation: it is incorrect that we must confine our artistic expression in order to get state support – we can really do whatever we want. That's what the state is proud of – that they dare to allow this.

The Schaubühne produces work of quality; in return the West Berlin Senate gives it generous subsidies because the theatre adds significantly to the prestige of West Berlin. In this respect, the Schaubühne contributes to the maintenance of the capitalist *status quo*; but then so does any academic whose work enhances the reputation of the "Free" University of West Berlin.

The latest step towards becoming "part of the cultural establishment" is the move to a magnificent new theatre financed by the West Berlin Senate. In the summer of 1974 Stein had already said that he regarded the stage at the Schaubühne as merely "provisional" (*Die Presse*, 12 June 1974), and two years later work began on renovating and adapting a building on the Kurfürstendamm in the heart of Berlin's "West End." It was an early cinema, designed in 1927 by the architect, Erich Mendelsohn, and purchased by the Berlin Senate as a monument to the architecture of the period. It was agreed that the Schaubühne should be rehoused in it at a cost now approaching 100 million DM (£25 million).

The new theatre designed by Jürgen Sawade is perhaps the most modern and flexible ever constructed. The whole area of the former cinema has been gutted to provide a supremely functional theatre building, allowing the possibility of one enormous performance space or of three separate auditoria. The area devoted to foyer and restaurant is only about a sixth that of the auditorium and stage area. As Peter Stein points out, it is more important for a theatre to create a place of performance than to provide vast areas where the public can drink coffee and be seen during the interval.

It is hoped that the new building will not only be considerably more practicable as a working space but will also provide new impulses for creativity. For there was something disturbing about the development of the decade at the Schaubühne. It had begun with the revolutionary optimism of Brecht's *The Mother* and – setting aside *The Oresteia*, with which it had been intended to open the Kurfürstendamm Schaubühne – the decade had ended with the desolate commentary on Western society of Strauss's *Great and Small*. As Stein confessed in November 1978 (quoted in *Theater heute* 1979/1, p. 16):

Of course it is basically true that the group that founded the new Schaubühne in 1970 and laid down new ways of working cannot grow old together.

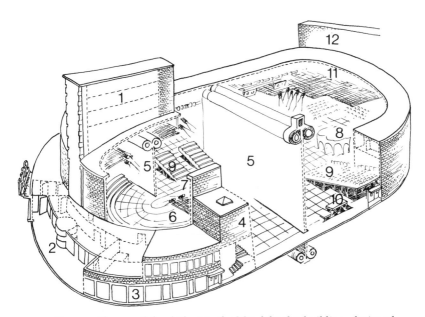

Fig. 11   The new Schaubühne in the Mendelssohn building, designed by Jürgen Sawade.
1   Administration
2   Foyer
3   Restaurant
4   Original facade conserved
5   Sound and fire-proof screens which can be lowered to create three separate auditoria:
    6   Amphitheatre (capacity 300)
    7   Middle auditorium (capacity app. 600)
    8   Main auditorium (capacity app. 600)
9   Audience seating which can be raised in sections
10 Floor sections (3 x 7 m) which can be individually raised to a height of 3.6 m
11 Lighting grid
12 Workshops, rehearsal space, etc.

Actors of thirty can form a group. If they put their minds to it, they can still manage at forty, but then sometime it's over. If you consider it in that perspective, it's clear that it can't work. Eight years are an enormously long time. Now we shall have to see how we can cope with this development. For some years things have been in a state of confusion. That is why people have left and come back. Really we should have blown the whole thing sky-high after seven years at most. Especially someone like me.

Inevitably, there will be those who regret the passing of the early years of the Schaubühne, the defiance, the adventure and the revolutionary commitment. As Stein has pointed out (*Göttinger Tageblatt,* 1 November 1975), the Schaubühne in 1970 deliberately did not employ any porters "because a porter is a symbol of working in an institution." But then keys got lost, people lost time waiting to get into the theatre or to lock up at night, and so on. The Schaubühne now employs three porters, a tiny indicator of the gradual institutionalization of the band of idealistic theatre people who gathered together in Berlin in the autumn of 1970.

The old Schaubühne sits amongst workers' tenement blocks; the underground railway, here running on an elevated section, rattles past within metres of its front door; the young porter in his untidy cubicle addresses you in the familiar "du" form; to see a rehearsal you may have to travel to a dirty disused cinema in the shadow of the Berlin Wall. Now the Schaubühne will move to the entertainment quarter of West Berlin, amongst night clubs and *cordon bleu* restaurants; Mercedes glide past in place of the *U-Bahn;* more tourists than workers wander down the broad pavements of the Kurfürstendamm.

As Peter Stein wryly observed to me on 18 October 1980:

The move to the Mendelssohn building which hasn't yet even taken place has already created colossal problems for us by getting us branded as a theatre that has been fossilized, absorbed into the establishment, and has sold out to bribes (and I am not saying that there might not be a grain of truth in this). Since this view of our work predates our move by a good two and a half years, the actual move itself will only present us with the opportunity of demonstrating the obvious, that is, that artistic work, including that of the theatre, does not depend on what street it is carried out in. The dangers that threaten us do not derive from the building in which we work and are always present as a potential menace.

It would be unrealistic to expect the Schaubühne to remain the same company it was in the early seventies. As it consolidated its achievements, its possibilities necessarily became fewer. From being an "emergent" group, to use Raymond Williams's terminology, it has become a part of the "dominant" theatre. This happened with the Moscow Art Theatre as with the Berliner Ensemble. Other groups, younger, more demanding, more idealistic, will take over the work and become the new pioneers, only in their turn to be replaced.

The fear for the Schaubühne is not that it will become an accepted part of the bourgeois entertainment scene of West Berlin, but that this acceptance will diminish the seriousness of their work and their critical analysis of society. It is hoped, however, that the new young actors who have joined the ensemble (Paul Burian, Roland Schäfer, Udo Samel) will give new life to work at the Schaubühne. Stein would also like to encourage the work of younger directors, but their efforts have been disappointing so far (the American Robert Wilson's *Death Destruction and Detroit* and Roland Schäfer's production of Schiller's *Die Räuber* (*The Robbers*), both in 1979, were dismal failures). As Stein admits, any attempt to engage further directors would involve reducing his leading role at the Schaubühne, "because a lot of people are simply uneasy about getting into my proximity" (*Theater heute*, 1979/1, p. 16).

Meanwhile, however, Stein will continue to resist any tendency to turn the Schaubühne into a monument (*ibid.*, p. 16):

This theatre could for example be a place of continuing research and show what is possible in terms of theatrical activities and actions. We could perform a definite function in communicating extreme and perhaps elitist forms of theatrical thought and feeling with a certain "common sense," that is, in a non-elitist manner. This is something I have always attempted and which one might reinforce.

Stein's latest work on *The Oresteia* of Aeschylus has maintained the function of the Schaubühne as "a place of continuing research" and has once again shown how a text, known only to an elite, is relevant to the experience and problems of our generation. This may not be theatre for the people, but at least it is theatre that has unflinchingly shown concern about the direction in which people are heading.

The value of the theatre as a political instrument does not lie in communicating facts nor in proposing solutions; its special quality is that it can examine in a unique way aspects of human experience which have helped to shape the consciousness of the audience: "it has the capacity to examine human qualities that direct politics or law cannot – such as death, irrationality, insanity . . . the subtle kinds of suppression, such as the workings of memory or myth in the human mind. Through theatre one can confront the past" (Stein, quoted in Lackner, *Drama Review*, T74 (1977) 88–9).

Stein regards his theatre as a means of liberating human potential,

28 Aeschylus' *Oresteia*. Clytemnestra (Edith Clever) stands over the mutilated bodies of Agamemnon and Cassandra.

as a way of removing mental blocks caused by false habits of thought and feeling. The artist in society (*Tasso*), the little man striving for greatness (*Peer Gynt*), the individual in relation to the state (*Homburg*), the search for a Utopia (*As You Like It*), all these perennial human situations were analysed afresh with the intention of freeing the audience (and the actors) from their inherited false conceptions. In this sense, Stein's theatre was not an attempt to destroy or replace the past but to conserve it: as Dieter Sturm said in an interview with Jack Zipes (*Theater*, vol. 9, no. 1 (1977) pp. 53–4):

We have come more and more to consider the theater as a kind of protesting moment that raises objections of a conservative kind. "Conservative" in the sense that we believe ourselves and sense ourselves to be living in a society which is suffering from an incredible loss of humanity and a great process of deprivation. Not only is there a curtailment of creativity, of subjective conditioning for all forms of rich imaginative creation, but also a complete amnesia regarding vast areas of human relations, in other words, a forgetting of human possibilities for action and development. However, we have also been convinced that this can be changed in some revolutionary or evolutionary sense, even by theater . . . insisting upon certain human possibilities, certain figurations of the human imagination, certain abilities of human beings to live, to move, to relate to one another, and insisting on this in images that are presently being demolished by this society and generally demolished not only by those forces which see themselves as conservative but just as much by those forces that see themselves as politically progressive.

In the same interview Stein explained what he understood by "conservatism" in this context (*ibid.*, pp. 54–6):

the possibility to feel, think, to see things together and to fantasize. The crucial thing for us – and the theater has this fantastic history – is the theater *in paradoxis*. Generally speaking, the paradox is a decisive element in the human activity of imagination.
   The theater has a . . . capacity for regulated paradox, for regulated, performed and controlled irrationality is part of theater . . . one can make contradictions clearly capable of being experienced and constantly reproducible and alive only in the theater.

For Stein, the decisive political act of theatre is a humanist one, just as Marx's philosophy has as its ultimate aim the restoration of human dignity to all men. An essential element of human experience is the ability to recognize and embrace contradictions, and while much left-wing political thinking dismisses such an ability as woolly-minded liberalism, for Stein it is central to life and his theatre: "I am firmly convinced that the encouragement of man's ability to be able to see and be aware of life's contradictions is quite important, so that he can experience within himself a certain abundance of life" (*Theater heute*, 1979/1, p. 16).

The particular contradiction which Stein has explored most fully is that of the individual's relationship to society. The theatre in this century has found itself in a contradictory situation: traditionally drama has centred on individual conflict, but now the whole concept of the individual has been thrown into question. The complexity of the modern state, improved communications, increasing industrialization, behavioural psychology, sociological analysis, all have made inroads on the concept of the individual. As Theodor Adorno wrote in an open letter to Rolf Hochhuth, author of plays which continue to make the obsolete assertion that individuals create history: "[This] has become a hideous mockery for those who were murdered in concentration camps or died in Vietnam . . . Hitler was a ham actor of misdeeds but not an individual" (*Theater heute*, 1967/7, pp. 1–2). Or as Dürrenmatt expressed it (*Theaterprobleme*, Arche, Zurich, 1973, p. 58): "Art only penetrates to the victims, if it penetrates to people at all; it can no longer reach the powerful. Creon's secretaries dispose of the case of Antigone."

Expressionist playwrights and Brecht explored the possibility of writing dramas without individuals. Anonymous types took the place of rounded characters; man as an essence gave way to man as a function. But still the theatre has not found a wholly satisfactory way of dispensing with the individual, of depicting mass movements in the way that the novel or the film can manage. As the young Communist writer Franz Xaver Kroetz said in 1973 (*Kürbiskern* 2, p. 335):

to write big scenes, mass scenes, to give thirty different workers lines that are not interchangeable, and all that in ten minutes, that is something I might be able to achieve in twenty years' time – if I'm lucky. I can't yet; those are my limits. I'm happy if I can do justice to three or four people in two hours . . . I consider the movement of the masses, the representation of the masses as one of the central problems of our dramatists, and in my opinion the solution is possible only by portraying the sum total of individuals.

Until such plays are written, Stein has had to content himself with turning back to plays that portray a central individual, but in which Stein has had the opportunity to show that the depicted concept of individuality is illusory. In *Tasso* the agonies of the suffering artist were shown to proceed from a social situation where his poetry was reduced to a consumer product for the delectation of the ruling class. In *Peer Gynt* Peer's untiring search for his own individuality was shown to be totally misguided; in the "Gyntian" sense, the true individuals were Begriffenfeldt's madmen, utterly isolated from one another by their total self-absorption; genuine individual meaning could only be achieved by becoming a part of the new rising class of the proletariat. In *Homburg* one saw how the Prince sacrificed his individuality to the military machine of the state and was carried away, a lifeless puppet. And so on, until Strauss's *Great and Small*, where Lotte's pursuit of herself ended in utter desolation.

None of these productions offered any practical solution to the sense of bourgeois alienation (although *Summerfolk* came near to implying one); there was no resolution of the contradiction between the tenacious belief in one's individuality and the recognition that that belief was largely founded on an obsolete view of life. But at least Peter Stein has unflinchingly recognized this contradiction and has explored its implications. This must be accounted a significant contribution to the theatre of our age.

The same quality of paradox has characterized Stein's theatrical aesthetics. For him the theatre offers a unique and contradictory experience: the closeness of the living actor combined with the distance created by the artificiality of the theatrical context (*Die Presse*, 12 June 1974):

Distance and scepticism are for me the basis of all work in the theatre. The fascinating part then comes in the dialectic between distance and closeness. If closeness dominates, there are exciting creative moments, if distance dominates there are beautiful insights. An evening in the theatre comes alive only through this tension, in these cross-currents between distance and closeness. If there is only distance, the essential theatrical impulses are destroyed; if there is only closeness, then it leaves behind a nausea as though one had eaten too much.

Despite his assertion that all his theatre work is political, he has – with the minor exception of Kelling's *The Altercation* – always avoided the closeness of commentary on immediate contemporary events (Protocol no. 502, 30 November 1975):

Theatrical reality – which we examined in the *Antiquity Project* and which we shall explore further in the Shakespeare project – consists of the reality portrayed by the actors, by those who create it. If you speak on stage in an immediate and direct manner about [actual] reality – and it must be remembered that the audience is also a part of that reality – theatre disappears . . . It is a matter of finding theatrical forms of debate about the reality that immediately surrounds us. We don't debate, we perform.

It has always been central to Stein's philosophy of theatre – and here he again shows himself to be Brecht's pupil – that the theatre should create distance in order to portray reality. Repeatedly he has preserved the historical "otherness" of his texts, from Schiller's *Intrigue and Love* to *The Oresteia*, always resisting any tendency to strive for a spurious topicality by updating the setting. The same distance is characteristic of his methods of staging: in his early productions the scenery confessed to its own theatricality (the two-dimensional ship of *Peer Gynt*, the painted clouds of *Optimistic Tragedy*); the properties were either real or blatantly artificial (the stuffed animals on wheels of *Peer Gynt*). Even when Stein moved more decisively in the direction of realism (*The Piggy Bank, Summerfolk, As You Like It*, the two Strauss plays), he did not employ realism in an attempt to trick the audience into accepting an illusion. Rather he pushed realism to its limits, to what he called "super-realism", so that the audience were at once invited to share in the stage illusion and to remain distanced from it. As Stein said in a post-production discussion of *Homburg* (Protocol no. 313, 14 April 1973):

We must attempt to represent realistic and psychological relationships not only precisely and accurately but also in a heightened manner, for example, to perform Chekhov not as Chekhov but as a kind of super-Chekhov. We must go a step further, that is, we must recognize and intensify the acting techniques that are appropriate to realism and take them beyond the limits of realism to discover any number of possibilities, to establish the limit of introducing as much fantasy and irrationality as possible in a realistic sphere of representation. That is, we must reach the ultimate limit of what is possible.

All Stein's work has been an exploration of what is possible in the theatre, and that is why it is meaningless to trace a clear line in his development. It is also a development that is almost certain to continue, for, as he has revealed, he carries with him a list of a whole variety of plays that he would one day like to direct (personal communication, 18 October 1980):

The list of plays I should like to direct is a long one. It has also changed in the light of recent changes in our ensemble. To give a few names, *Faust*, of course, *Richard II*, a Chekhov (perhaps a complete version of *Platonov*), *The Mountain Giants* [by Pirandello] (if one were permitted to write a conclusion for it), *The Temptation of St. Anthony* by Flaubert or perhaps none of these.

The decision to direct a certain play does not follow any ideological or aesthetic programme but results from the impulses of a given situation (*Travail théâtral*, 1972, p. 22):

the decision to stage a certain play has, for me, always arisen from the work situation I found myself in. It has been this way up till now. For each new show I always choose the one which I think will allow me to overcome or modify radically the difficulties which I encountered during the previous one.

Once having chosen a play and gained the ensemble's approval for it, Stein's next step, where appropriate, is to inform himself fully about the text and its background and to arrange for his actors to do likewise. He insists that he never develops a conception in advance: "There are only groping experiments before the rehearsal, a series of arguments and questionings in order to set up a play and transmit it to the actors so that they too can pose questions and then use the information for their work" (*Performance* 4 (1972), 75). In place of a fixed conception, Stein engages with his actors in what he has called a "doubting process" (*Theater*, Vol. 9, no. 1 (1977), 52). The lengthy preparations, which are now not pursued with the same intensity as in the early days of the Schaubühne, have been regarded by some members of the ensemble as irksome. After a seminar paper read by the *Dramaturg* Ellen Hammer during work on the *Antiquity Project*, Bruno Ganz got up and said that such academic research was boring and that he could not take any more of it, and one imagines that most British and American actors would sympathize with him. But Stein insists that such research is essential: "If you want to dig a hole, it's no good saying 'It's boring always digging at the same spot. Let's dig all round it!' But then you never dig a hole" (unpublished Bergmann interview, 1978).

Eventually, after the period of preparation, when the level of information can be expected to be roughly equal, discussion turns to casting. While these discussions proceed on democratic lines, they are dominated by the judgment of Stein, who insists on a hierarchy of actors: "I am convinced that in a certain context some act better than others. In a different context these others might be able to act better but they'll hardly ever act well" (*ibid.*). In the context of the Schaubühne with its four productions a year, Stein's insistence on giving the major parts to his best actors means two things: first, the weaker members of the ensemble remain weak, having little chance to develop, and some, like Gerd David and Hans Joachim Diehl, have become so disillusioned that they have given up acting altogether. Secondly, the long collaboration between Stein and a handful of regular actors has led to a state of dependence on Stein which is not entirely healthy. Other directors, with the exception of Grüber, have had difficulties in entering this tight-knit family, of which Stein describes himself ironically as the "Super-Daddy" (*ibid.*). For over ten years now, Jutta Lampe, Edith Clever, Michael König and Werner Rehm have acted regularly with Stein. Clever left the Schaubühne for a while only to return. Of the original Schaubühne core, Bruno Ganz alone has managed to free himself entirely, but, significantly, by working in the cinema not at another theatre, and Stein still has "desperate hopes that he some time will again act in the theatre, and do it in collaboration with me and with us" (*Theater heute,* 1979/1, p. 16). Rüdiger Hacker once summarized the sense of dependence felt by many members of the ensemble when he said (Protocol no. 490, 1 September 1975) that he "had the feeling that he had been married to the Schaubühne for the last five years without however having the pleasure of sexual intercourse."

One of the major reasons that actors enjoy working with Stein so much, to the point that they can hardly tolerate another director, is due to the energy and care with which he conducts rehearsals. Each actor knows that every move and intonation will be noted by Stein to be accepted or rejected, that he or she will be observed with the attention and respect normally granted only by one's lovers. Rehearsals with Stein are therefore almost always a rewarding experience, a period of thoughtful exploration and themselves almost theatrical occasions. For Stein is something of a performer himself: the quality of his acting could be seen when he took part in *The Havana Hearing* and when, at short notice, he had to replace Rüdiger Hacker as Le Beau in *As You Like It.* He was particularly impressive while rehearsing Shakespeare: as someone remarked, he would have made an excellent Rosalind. Like Peter Brook, however, Stein cannot understand how an intelligent person can be an actor, obliged to repeat the same performance again and again.

Instead, Stein performs during rehearsals. His energy and enthusiasm are considerable. He will enter a rehearsal, apparently organizing half a dozen things at once, firing remarks in various languages (he speaks fluent English, French and Italian) and infecting everyone with his own vitality. During the rehearsal he will pass witty comments, shout encouragement, coax gently and utter obscenities by turn.

His approach to rehearsals is to begin by inviting the actors to offer something to him: "Most of all I love to watch the actors work – just watching and making observations is my favourite kind of rehearsal" (quoted in Lackner, *Drama Review,* T74 (1977), 82). "I'm one-hundred-percent dependent upon what I see. Before I perceive what goes on between two actors, or three, or four, I can't say anything about it. I'm totally unable to offer any suggestions before the fact. That's why I'm especially observant of the actors' peculiarities and method of work during the rehearsals" (*Performance* 4 (1972), 73). He normally never dictates moves to an actor, regarding this as the responsibility of the actor, as part of his "trade." Only in the tense atmosphere of *As You Like It* did he insist on certain moves. Usually, however, his method is to receive impulses from the actor and then to encourage him or her to develop something further.

Therese Giehse (*"Ich hab nichts zum Sagen"*, pp. 196–7) spoke of Stein's gentleness in rehearsals and told how he had once solved the technical problem of a set-change in *The Mother*. He stacked the furniture which had to be brought on to stage in a certain way, turned to the scene-shifters and said: "That should do it."

He said it in a friendly matter-of-fact way. He didn't try to show off his superior knowledge. Simply helpful, he said: "That should do it." The stagehands looked somewhat crestfallen at what Stein had shown them, then said: "Yes, that should do it." What a fuss other directors would have made. How they'd have shown off their superiority! People with real talent are modest.

Stein is an expert diagnostician and can unerringly sense when a scene is not working. With seemingly total concentration he will isolate a gesture or a piece of intonation that does not fit and will seek with the actors a means of removing the problem. Above all, he is concerned to clarify, to be able to understand at any given moment why a character is speaking or behaving in a certain way. Where a scene is going well, such conscious analysis is problematic. To examine too closely why something is working on stage may destroy its spontaneity and prevent the subconscious achievement from being recaptured. On the other hand, actors seek for informed praise and may need to know why they have done well so that they can repeat the same performance even when the initial inspiration has gone (as was the case in the Natalie/Elector scene in *Homburg*).

Where any scene is going badly, Stein never makes use of theatre games or structured improvisation, but tries to identify and correct the difficulties. He will even invite an actor to work "from the outside in" in order to get a move or a line right: "Don't be afraid to do something externally or mechanically. That way you might arrive at the feeling" (*Great and Small* rehearsal, 7 October 1978). He will also get up and demonstrate a suggestion, but never acting it out fully, so that the actor is merely given an indication of a move and is then allowed to make it his own. When an actor fails to respond to one of Stein's proposals, he persists with extreme patience until he notices that the actor cannot get there, for the time being at least. He does not bully his actors nor push them beyond their own limits, so that they are seldom demoralized. As he said to Jack Zipes: "From the very beginning we have always demanded as much as possible from the actors, up to the breaking point. But, if they cannot pull something off, then we drop it" (*Theater*, vol. 9, no. 1 (1977), p. 51). Characteristic of this attitude was the following exchange at a rehearsal of *Great and Small* on 7 October 1978 after some fifteen minutes spent by Elke Petri on the intonation of a single line: Stein: "Have you understood what I'm saying?" Petri: "Yes." Stein: "Then that's all right."

With such an experienced and willing actress as Petri such patience and trust is productive. Stein is at his worst, however, with poor actors. He readily admits that "I have great difficulty with people who aren't serious" (*Performance* 4 (1972), 75). If there is nothing coming from the actors he becomes bored and irritable. He is little help to actors who offer nothing, for he feels that they should have learnt their skills before coming to work with him. Where an actor seems obstinate or lazy, Stein shows no mercy, becoming coarse and aggressive. Stein cares desperately about the process of acting and cannot bear to have his time or the time of others wasted by incompetence. For, despite the lavishness of many of Stein's productions, the actor is central to his theatre: "Technical effects . . . are an optional extra . . . You can for example watch *Summerfolk* on the rehearsal stage, lit by two floods, and you will see what is essential and decisive" (*Der Tagesspiegel*, 12 October 1975).

The organization of the rehearsal schedule would strike most British and American directors as predictably Teutonic in the sense that Stein will not permit a run-through of the play until each section of it has been worked through in considerable detail. The main disadvantage is that it is only at the very end of the rehearsal process that an actor can acquire an immediate sense of the overall development of his role; until then he has to work piecemeal like the film actor whose part is made up of a series of "takes." Stein's defence of his method, however, is eloquent (personal communication, 18 October 1980):

I make it a principle never to have run-throughs until the whole play has been worked through, i.e. immediately before the opening night. The practice of English theatres you describe, which I find terrible and which in Germany too is taken for granted by incompetent directors, seems to me the reason why many Anglo-Saxon theatre productions appear so slick.

As with his directing style, it would be impossible to generalize about the acting style he has discovered with the Schaubühne ensemble, since it has varied from the *plakativ*, demonstrational style of *Optimistic Tragedy* to the psychological realism of *Summerfolk*. The clearest statement Stein has made regarding the style of his actors dates from 1972 (*Travail théâtral*, p. 30):

Let us say that this style of acting rests on a lively use of the theories of Brecht and the principles of Kortner. It results in a performing style which is both descriptive and narrative, which relates, shows, presents but which does not renounce the possibility of exploring psychic and theatrical events by means of empathy nor abandons tension – something that is very important to us. And this style remains capable of demonstrating that the actor demonstrates, of revealing the actual working process, the fact that the actor offers a gesture, an intonation, an idea – and all this without falling into abstraction nor lessening the reality of the events that take place on stage.

In terms of acting style, too, Stein willingly embraces and explores contradictions, in this case the demonstrational style of Brecht and the theatre of empathy. Where have these explorations led? What in fact are Stein's achievements as a director that justify the subtitle of this book?

Stein would not regard himself as a theatrical genius: "I'm a totally ordinary person, I'm unmarried, I like football and television like anyone else" (*Stuttgarter Nachrichten*, 18 June 1973). After *Peer Gynt* he said of himself: "I'm not very imaginative" (Protocol no. 107, 26 May 1971), and at times during rehearsals on *As You Like It* he decided that he was not really a director at all. As he said in a radio discussion on 23 December 1975: "I always have certain difficulties in understanding myself, difficulties of understanding myself as a director. A director – that would be more in the sense of someone arrogant, fascinating, radiating genius, his head full of images and visions, which are then transmitted in a mysterious way so that the actors burst into flower under this visionary spell" (quoted in *Die Zeit*, 2 January 1976). This is not the kind of director that Stein is, although, without the ironical exaggeration, the description fits his colleague, Klaus Michael Grüber. It is also not the kind of director that Stein would wish to be. Despite his modest assertions and the passive role he adopts initially in rehearsals, Stein is a highly inventive and imaginative person, but he has always distrusted the randomness of the imagination. As early as 1968 he said in discussion with Zadek: "Imagination is not something that comes down to us from above or floats in space, but imagination is basically the product of the consciousness which each individual has attained or received or been indoctrinated with" (*Theater heute*, 1968/13, p. 26). And to Jack Zipes he spoke of his doubts about "the role of the so-called 'sudden flash,' the inspiration," and said: "if nothing occurs to you, the least you can be is precise" (*Theater*, vol. 9, no. 1 (1977), p. 53).

It is this precision and clarity that has distinguished Stein's work and must be accounted one of his major achievements. He has taken classics that had acquired the patina of museum exhibits and, "examining each word for its actual – not literary – meaning" (Lackner, p. 92), has lent them vividness and freshness. Through his employment of distancing techniques he has blown away the cobwebs of mystification that surrounded plays both old and new and has held them up to his audiences for both immediate enjoyment and critical assessment. This theatre of precision and clarity does not suit all tastes. Peter Zadek, whose own productions depend on brilliant, outrageous and often totally arbitrary ideas (his *The Winter's Tale* was performed on two tons of green slime) and who, significantly, began his directing career in England, is particularly outspoken about the polished and thought-out precision of Stein's work. He has compared Stein's actors to vegetables that have been cooked so long that they have lost all their flavour and he asserts that he would rather watch second-rate amateurs, because at least their unpredictability is theatrical. In an interview in 1978 (quoted in *Theater heute*, 1979/1, p. 15) Zadek spoke of "the brilliant work of Peter Stein which always concentrates on absolute stylization, on the utterly perfect statement. After a while the people in his plays no longer interest me. I find that boring."

Unlike Zadek and Grüber, Stein will not astonish audiences by the boldness of his vision, but, in a world that is endangered more and more by the misleading use of words and images in the media, there must be a significant place for a theatre which resists this and which strives to replace such mystification with clarity.

Moreover, Stein's pursuit of clarity has not led him to create a cold, analytical theatre but a theatre of refined beauty: "I believe that destroying aesthetic values would lead to a gigantic loss of consciousness. And that would be of no help to any side and no use to anyone" (*Theater heute*, 1968/13, p. 27). In many respects he has rediscovered the aesthetic enjoyment of Max Reinhardt's theatre (most obviously in *As You Like It*), without, however, indulging in the sheer sensual pleasure of Reinhardt's productions. To have brought together the clarity and political relevance of Brecht with the aesthetic satisfaction of Reinhardt is no mean achievement.

The final act of synthesis which makes Stein one of the most significant directors working in the theatre today is his drawing on usable elements from two totally opposed theatrical styles, on the one hand, the rational, narrative, demonstrational style associated with Brecht and, on the other, the irrational, empathetic style which has its most extreme manifestation in Artaud and his followers. Several attempts have been made to achieve a synthesis between these two major trends in progressive theatre, as in Peter Weiss's *Marat/Sade*, but they are ideologically at odds; for Brecht's theatre

Table 2. *Opposing tendencies in directing style*

Alienation	Empathy
Rationality	Irrationality
History	Myth
Distance	Immediacy
Demonstration	Embodiment
Conscious analysis	Subconscious intuition
Narration	Description
Clarity	Mystification
Physical presentation	Psychic realization
Cf. Brecht's *Lehrstücke*	Cf. Artaud's Theatre of Cruelty

proposes a historical view of man as alterable, whereas the Theatre of Cruelty depends on a mythical view of man as an unchanging constant. Clearly, Stein sides with Brecht, but equally clearly he recognizes and is fascinated by the irrational impulses in man. Thus he will explore plays that are "ideologically unsound," not in order to denounce them in advance but to experience them fully in order to be aware of what elements in them are to be denounced. Peer Gynt's search for his individuality, the search in *As You Like It* for a Utopia, these are shown to be illusory, but only after they have been communicated fully and convincingly by the actors. It is as though with each play the audience undergoes an educative process: as in *As You Like It* we are led through a dark labyrinth to a beautiful and mythical illusion – but are ultimately shown that it is an illusion.

In the *Prinz von Homburg* programme Strauss spoke of the "dream" conception of the piece: "This is not a dream in deepest sleep – not a play about the 'distorted' visions of the unconscious mind – but a clear, logical dream-construction, hovering in equilibrium." In the dream image Stein has found an eminently theatrical means of synthesizing observable reality with the irrational. The quality of the dream is not that it is full of distorted expressionist images. Usually the images are intensely clear and real; it is their juxtaposition that is felt to be unreal and disturbing. So at the end of the picnic scene of *Summerfolk,* in the dream sequence of *As You Like It,* in the trivially real but haunting images of the Botho Strauss pieces, Stein has used realistic devices in a constellation that goes beyond the description of a moment to the super-realism he had been seeking.

Stein would be the first to insist that he is merely an explorer in this territory and that he has not penetrated very far: "Starting from the hope that perhaps everything can be achieved in the theatre, we have of course arrived at the conclusion that not so terribly much has been achieved" (*Theater heute*, 1979/1, p. 16). That "not so terribly much," however, consists of a series of almost entirely successful productions, of a consistently clear and precise style of direction, of the restoration of beauty to committed theatre, and of the beginnings of synthesis in the divergent strains of modern theatre. Most important of all, Stein the explorer clearly has no intention of stopping where he is.

Stein would also insist that he is not alone in his explorations, indeed that they are only possible within the structure of the Schaubühne: "We are mutually dependent on each other to arrive at reasonable ideas. Only the general involvement of all participants can prevent a lack of imagination from being replaced with committed intellectualism, which would surely be a catastrophe" (*Stuttgarter Zeitung*, 14 February 1975).

Over the years democratic participation at the Schaubühne has been considerably modified, but the essential core, the involvement of the actors in decision-making on productions, has remained. There are many reasons why the Schaubühne cannot act as a model. It enjoys a unique situation in being a private theatre receiving colossal subsidies from public funds. One can admire the wisdom of the West Berlin Senate and agree with Stein that, even if the Schaubühne were to throw all its subsidies out of the window, it would be better spent than on a Starfighter (*Travail théâtral*, 1972, p. 36). But, short of a radical change in attitude towards the financing of the theatre in English-speaking countries, there is little hope that a small, manoeuvrable and independent theatre might be as well supported as the Schaubühne. The money the Schaubühne receives (and this is still only one third the amount granted annually to the Berlin opera house) is not essential for the cost of productions, because it could still be an excellent and progressive theatre with less lavish stagings. The money is, however, important to allow a standing ensemble to be created that has the time to read, discuss and experiment together in addition to participating in lengthy rehearsals which slowly and painstakingly arrive at production decisions.

The freedom of the Schaubühne to present annually only four productions which represent its own interests rather than what is obviously attractive to the public, also depends on it being in a city large enough to provide a specialized audience consisting mainly of young intellectuals. It would be very difficult to imitate the Schaubühne model in an area where there was not a larger theatre catering for more conservative tastes.

Finally, the Schaubühne is a special case in that it has been able to collect together theatre workers that combine talent, intelligence and a degree of political commitment. Quite apart from the intellectual capacity and articulacy of actors like Clever, Lampe and König, and the willingness of Stein to share his investigations with them, it is, for example, a delight and a surprise to find how much a costume-designer like Moidele Bickel also contributes to the theoretical considerations of the Schaubühne.

Perhaps it is the structure that has helped the actors to respond as they do; perhaps it is a surprise that a costume-designer contributes so many ideas only because costume-designers are seldom asked to express their views on a production. And it is in this respect that the Schaubühne can operate as a model of great significance (*Performance* 4 (1972), 75–6):

I don't think the Schaubühne can be a model for organizational form, but it is a model of an approach through exact investigation and examination of the plays and their themes, of scientific methodology in the preparatory work, of detail and precision and seriousness by everyone taking part as much as possible in the process of conscious development.

Where in the English-speaking world is there a company that so much as approaches this model? And even if there are not the subsidies available to make this a possibility, is there not still a place for a greater degree of democracy in any theatrical undertaking? Democracy, however, can only function where the level of information is roughly equal for actors and director alike. Actors – and costume-designers – will continue to be treated as executants of the director's vision unless they can argue rationally about the way a text should be approached; and directors will have only puppets at their disposal until they dare to encourage participation in their decisions. To work best, such democracy needs time but, even in the three-week rehearsal period of the average provincial company, preparatory reading and two days' preliminary discussion would be time well invested. Paradoxically such democratic debate does not weaken the role of the director but strengthens it immeasurably. The achievements of Peter Stein, Germany's leading theatre director, bear witness to that.

Theatre productions of Peter Stein

(not including film, television or opera)

indicates an invitation to the Berlin Theatre Festival

WERKRAUMTHEATER DER KAMMERSPIELE, MUNICH

Saved (Gerettet) by Edward Bond, adapted by Martin Sperr (West German première)

Première: 15 April 1967
Dramaturg: Ivan Nagel
Design (set and costumes): Jürgen Rose
Cast: Len – Michael König; Pam – Jutta Schwarz; Fred – Christian Doermer

BREMER THEATER

Kabale und Liebe (Intrigue and Love) by Friedrich Schiller   22 performances

Première: 7 November 1967
Design: Jürgen Rose
Cast: Ferdinand – Michael König; Luise – Edith Clever; Lady Milford – Jutta Lampe; President – Kurt Hübner; Wurm – Bruno Ganz

WERKRAUMTHEATER DER KAMMERSPIELE, MUNICH

Im Dickicht der Städte (In the Jungle of Cities) by Bertolt Brecht
                                                                20 performances

Première: 9 March 1968
Design: Karl-Ernst Herrmann
Music: Peter Fischer
Cast: Shlink – Hans Korte; Garga – Bruno Ganz; Marie – Edith Clever; Wurm – Dieter Laser

Viet Nam Diskurs (Vietnam-Discourse) by Peter Weiss   6 performances

(co-directed with Wolfgang Schwiedrzik)
Première: 5 July 1968
Design: F. Lechenperg-Recker
Music: Peter Fischer
Cast: Compère – Wolfgang Neuss

BREMER THEATER

Torquato Tasso by Johann Wolfgang von Goethe   72 performances

Première: 30 March 1969
Dramaturg: Yaak Karsunke
Design: Wilfried Minks
Cast: Tasso – Bruno Ganz; Princess – Jutta Lampe; Leonore – Edith Clever;
    Duke – Wolfgang Schwarz; Antonio – Werner Rehm

SCHAUSPIELHAUS ZURICH

Early Morning by Edward Bond (German première)

Première: 2 October 1969
Dramaturg: Klaus Völker
Design: Uwe Lausen, Günter Kuschmann
Costumes: Susanne Raschig
Cast: Victoria – Joana Maria Gorvin; Albert – Wolfgang Reichmann; Arthur
    – Bruno Ganz; George – Dieter Laser; Len – Tilo Prückner; Joyce – Ingrid
    Burkhard; Florence Nightingale – Jutta Lampe

Cock-a-Doodle Dandy (*Kikeriki*) by Sean O'Casey   26 performances

(co-directed with Ulrich Heising)
Première: 6 December 1969
Dramaturg: Klaus Völker
Design: Karl Kneidl
Cast: Mahan – Klaus Löwitsch; Marthraun – Dieter Laser; Loreleen – Hanna
    Schygulla; Father Domineer – Bruno Ganz

The Changeling by Thomas Middleton and William Rowley (German
première)   19 performances

Première: 11 June 1970
Dramaturg: Dieter Sturm
Design: Wilfried Minks
Costumes: Susanne Raschig
Cast: Beatrice – Edith Clever; De Flores – Bruno Ganz

SCHAUBÜHNE AM HALLESCHEN UFER, WEST BERLIN

Die Mutter (*The Mother*) by Bertolt Brecht after the novel by Gorky
68 performances

(co-directed with Wolfgang Schwiedrzik and Frank-Patrick Steckel)
Première: 8 October 1970
Dramaturg: Dieter Sturm
Music: Hanns Eisler, rehearsed by Peter Fischer

Design: Klaus Weiffenbach
Costumes: Susanne Raschig, Joachim Herzog
Cast: Pelagea Wlassowa – Therese Giehse; Pawel – Heinrich Giskes; Teacher
    – Günter Lampe

Das Verhör von Habana (*The Havana Hearing*) by Hans-Magnus
Enzensberger

(collective production)
Première: 2 February 1971

Die Auseinandersetzung (*The Altercation*) by Gerhard Kelling

27 performances

(Workers' and Apprentices' Theatre)
Première: 6 February 1971

*Peer Gynt by Henrik Ibsen   158 performances

Première: 13–14 May 1971
Dramaturg: Botho Strauss
Music: Peter Fischer
Design: Karl-Ernst Herrmann
Costumes: Moidele Bickel, Susanne Raschig, Joachim Herzog
Masks: Ricarda Poppy, Ulrich Hilbert
Cast: Peer 1 – Heinrich Giskes; Peer 2 – Michael König; Peer 3 – Bruno Ganz;
    Peer 4 – Wolf Redl; Peer 5 – Dieter Laser; Peer 6 – Wolf Redl; Peer 7 –
    Werner Rehm; Peer 8 – Bruno Ganz; Solveig – Jutta Lampe; Aase – Edith
    Clever; Ingrid – Sabine Andreas; Woman in Green – Rita Leska; Troll King
    – Otto Sander; Anitra – Angela Winkler; Dr Begriffenfeldt – Hans Joachim
    Diehl; Strange Passenger – Klaus-Harald Kuhlmann; Buttonmoulder/
    Engineer – Claus Gärtner

Optimistische Tragödie (*Optimistic Tragedy*) by Vsevolod Vishnevsky

27 performances

Première: 18 April 1972
Dramaturgen: Dieter Sturm, Frank-Patrick Steckel
Music: Peter Fischer
Design: Klaus Weiffenbach
Costumes: Susanne Raschig
Cast: Commissar – Elke Petri; Anarchist leader – Peter Fitz; Hoarse-Voice –
    Otto Sander; Alexei – Ulrich Wildgruber; Commander – Rüdiger Hacker

*Prinz Friedrich von Homburg (*Kleists Traum vom Prinzen Homburg – Kleist's
Dream of Prince Homburg*) by Heinrich von Kleist   147 performances

Première: 4 November 1972
Dramaturg: Botho Strauss

Set: Karl-Ernst Herrmann
Costumes: Moidele Bickel
Cast: Homburg – Bruno Ganz; Elector – Peter Lühr; Electress – Katharina Tüschen; Princess Natalie – Jutta Lampe; Hohenzollern – Werner Rehm; Kottwitz – Otto Sander

*Fegefeuer in Ingolstadt (Purgatory in Ingolstadt) by Marieluise Fleisser
58 performances

Première: 19 December 1972
Dramaturg: Frank-Patrick Steckel
Design: Karl-Ernst Herrmann
Costumes: Joachim Herzog
Cast: Roelle – Rüdiger Hacker; Olga – Angela Winkler; Berotter – Otto Mächtlinger; Clementine – Sabine Andreas

*Das Sparschwein (La Cagnotte – The Piggy Bank) by Eugène Labiche, translated by Botho Strauss
133 performances

Première: 1 September 1973
Dramaturg: Jean Jourdheuil (with Botho Strauss)
Design: Karl-Ernst Herrmann
Costumes: Susanne Raschig
Cast: Champbourcy – Otto Sander; Léonida – Jutta Lampe; Colladan – Wolf Redl; Cordenbois – Werner Rehm; Blanche – Elke Petri; Félix – Willem Menne; Baucantin – Otto Mächtlinger

*Antikenprojekt I (Antiquity Project I)
29 performances

Première: 6 February 1974
Dramaturg: Frank-Patrick Steckel
Design: Karl-Ernst Herrmann
Costumes, Masks: Moidele Bickel
Music: Peter Fischer
Practical instructors: Gerd Kaminski, Miloslav Lipinsky
Cast: Andreas, Ganz, Clever, König, Jutta Lampe, Petri, Tüschen, Winkler, Fitz, Giskes, Hacker, Mächtlinger, Sander, Feik, etc.

Die Unvernünftigen sterben aus (They Are Dying Out) by Peter Handke
43 performances

Première: 6 June 1974
Design: Klaus Weiffenbach
Costumes: Moidele Bickel
Cast: Quitt – Bruno Ganz; Quitt's Wife – Angela Winkler; Paula Tax – Sabine Andreas

Sommergäste (*Summerfolk*) by Maxim Gorky   135 performances

Première: 22 December 1974
Dramaturgen: Botho Strauss, Ellen Hammer
Design: Karl-Ernst Herrmann
Costumes: Susanne Raschig
Cast: Bassov – Wolf Redl; Varvara – Edith Clever; Vlas – Michael König; Suslov – Otto Sander; Yulia – Elke Petri; Dudakov – Werner Rehm; Olga – Sabine Andreas; Shalimov – Bruno Ganz (later replaced by Peter Fitz); Maria Lvovna – Jutta Lampe; Dvoetochie – Günter Lampe

Shakespeare's Memory   80 performances

Première: 22–23 December 1976
Dramaturg: Dieter Sturm
Design: Karl-Ernst Herrmann
Costumes: Moidele Bickel, Susanne Raschig, Joachim Herzog
Cast: Andreas, Engel, Hacker, König, Günter Lampe, Jutta Lampe, Mächtlinger, Menne, Petri, Redl, Rehm, Sander, Libgart Schwarz, etc.

As You Like It (*Wie es euch gefällt*) by William Shakespeare

117 performances

Première: 20 September 1977
Dramaturgen: Ellen Hammer, Dieter Sturm
Design: Karl-Ernst Herrmann
Costumes: Moidele Bickel
Music: Peter Michael Hamel
Cast: Rosalind – Jutta Lampe; Orlando – Michael König; Touchstone – Werner Rehm; Celia – Tina Engel; Jaques – Peter Fitz; Duke – Günter Lampe; Frederick – Otto Sander; Phebe – Elke Petri; Silvius – Wolf Redl; Audrey – Libgart Schwarz

Trilogie des Wiedersehens (*Trilogy of Return*) by Botho Strauss

107 performances

Première: 21 March 1978
Design: Karl-Ernst Herrmann
Costumes: Dagmar Niefind
Cast: Susanne – Libgart Schwarz; Moritz – Peter Fitz; Franz – Otto Mächtlinger; Elfriede – Elke Petri; Lothar – Werner Rehm; Ruth – Edith Clever; Marlies – Tina Engel; Felix – Roland Schäfer; Richard – Otto Sander; Peter – Paul Burian

Gross und klein (*Great and Small*) by Botho Strauss (World première)

129 performances

Première: 8 December 1978
Design: Karl-Ernst Herrmann

Costumes: Moidele Bickel
Cast: Lotte – Edith Clever (with Willem Menne, Elke Petri, Jutta Lampe, etc.)

The Oresteia by Aeschylus

Première: 18 October 1980
Design: Karl-Ernst Herrmann
Costumes: Moidele Bickel
Cast: Clytemnestra – Edith Clever; Agamemnon – Gunter Berger; Cassandra
  – Elke Petri; Orestes – Udo Samel; Electra – Tina Engel; Aegisthus – Peter
  Fitz; Pylades – Greger Hansen; Apollo – Peter Simonischek; Athene – Jutta
  Lampe

Bibliography

GENERAL WORKS AND ARTICLES

Canaris, Volker. "Zeit für Klassiker?" *Theater heute*, Velber bei Hannover, 1974/13, pp. 30–5.

Daiber, Hans. *Deutsches Theater seit 1945*, Reclam, Stuttgart, 1976.

Hayman, Ronald (ed.). *The German theatre*, Oswald Wolff, London, 1975.

Iden, Peter. *Die Schaubühne am Halleschen Ufer 1970–1979*, Hanser, Munich, 1979.

Innes, C. D., *Modern German drama*, Cambridge University Press, 1979.

Jäger, Gerd, Michaelis, Rolf, and Rischbieter, Henning. "An der Spitze: Die Schaubühne am Halleschen Ufer Berlin," *Theater heute*, Velber bei Hannover, 1973/13, pp. 12–50.

Kott, Jan. *Shakespeare our contemporary*, Methuen, London, 1965.

Kreuzer, Helmut (ed.). *Deutsche Dramaturgie der sechziger Jahre*, Max Niemeyer, Tübingen, 1974.

Lackner, Peter. "Peter Stein," *Drama Review*, New York, T74 (1977), 79–102.

Patterson, Michael. *German theatre today*, Pitman Publishing, London, 1976.

Rorrison, Hugh. "Berlin's democratic theatre and its *Peer Gynt*," *Theatre Quarterly*, London, vol. 4, no. 13 (1974), pp. 15–36.

Rühle, Günther. "Signatur am Ende des Weges. Erste Betrachtung nach zehn Jahren – Die Schlussbilder in Peter Steins Inszenierungen – Anmerkungen zu einer Stilfigur," *Frankfurter Allgemeine Zeitung*, 26 April 1978.

Sandmeyer, Peter. *Voraussetzungen und Möglichkeiten kollektiven Berufstheaters in Deutschland. Eine Untersuchung an hand der ersten Spielzeit des Theaterkollektivs der Schaubühne am Halleschen Ufer in Berlin (West)*, published doctoral dissertation, Freie Universität, Berlin, 1974.

Zipes, Jack. "Ends and beginnings. West German theater now," *Performance*, Fort Worth, 4 (1972) 54–62.

"The irresistible rise of the Schaubühne am Halleschen Ufer; a retrospective of the West Berlin theater collective," *Theater*, New Haven, vol. 9, no. 1 (1977), pp. 7–49.

DOCUMENTATION OF MAJOR PRODUCTIONS (IN CHRONOLOGICAL ORDER)

Saved: *Theater heute*, 1967/13, pp. 57–76.

Tasso: Goethe *et al. Torquato Tasso. Regiebuch der Bremer Inszenierung*, ed. Volker Canaris, Suhrkamp, Frankfurt am Main, 1970.

Theater heute, 1969/13, pp. 20–31.

178

Die Mutter: Brecht, Bertolt. *Die Mutter. Regiebuch der Schaubühnen-Inszenierung,* ed. Volker Canaris, Suhrkamp, Frankfurt am Main, 1971.
See also: Sandmeyer, pp. 111–25.
Peer Gynt: Hammer, Ellen, Herrmann, Karl-Ernst, and Strauss, Botho (eds.). *Peer Gynt. Ein Schauspiel aus dem neunzehnten Jahrhundert. Dokumentation der Schaubühnen-Inszenierung,* Schaubühne and Hentrich Verlag, Berlin, 1971.
Theater heute, 1971/6, pp. 16–19; 1971/13, pp. 18–39, 70–1.
See also: Rorrison, pp. 22–35; Sandmeyer, pp. 141–61.
Optimistic Tragedy: Theater heute, 1973/13, pp. 18–23.
Prinz Friedrich von Homburg: Theater heute, 1973/13, pp. 30–5.
Summerfolk: Mairowitz, David Zane. "Peter Stein's Summerfolk," *Plays and Players,* London, vol. 24, no. 8 (1977), pp. 18–21.
Rischbieter, Henning. "Peter Stein's Gorky. A review of *Summerfolk* in West Berlin," *Yale/theatre,* New Haven, Winter 1976, pp. 109–13. (First published *Theater heute,* 1975/2, pp. 20–3.)
Shakespeare's Memory: Programme, 18 pp. with 11 diagrams.
Theater heute, 1977/2, pp. 19–22.
See also: Lackner, pp. 79–102.
As You Like It: Mairowitz, David Zane. "As they like it," *Plays and Players,* London, vol. 25, no. 3 (1977), pp. 16–19.
Theater heute 1977/11, pp. 11–16.

MAJOR INTERVIEWS WITH AND STATEMENTS BY PETER STEIN (IN CHRONOLOGICAL ORDER)

"Drei Gesichtspunkte bei der Regie" (on *Saved*), *Theater heute,* 1967/13, pp. 74–5. (Reprinted in: Kreuzer, pp. 67–72).
"Was kann man machen?" *Theater heute,* 1968/13, pp. 26–9. (Reprinted in: Kreuzer, pp. 130–7).
"Die kollektive Bühne," *Christ und Welt,* Stuttgart, 4 September 1970.
"Warten auf die Zeitgenossen," *Frankfurter Neue Presse,* 3 October 1970.
"Bei uns wird niemand zu etwas gezwungen," *BZ,* Berlin, 18 January 1971.
"Polit-Theater, aber wie?" *Konkret,* Hamburg, 28 January 1971.
"La Schaubühne am Halleschen Ufer" (interview by Bernard Dort), *Travail théâtral,* Lausanne, 1972, pp. 16–36.
"The collective impulse" (interview by Jack Zipes), *Performance,* Fort Worth, 4 (1972), 69–76.
"Positionen und Probleme am Halleschen Ufer" (an interview with Peter Stein, Franz Rueb and Frank-Patrick Steckel by Oskar Neumann), *Kürbiskern,* Munich, 2 (1973), 335–47.
"Von heute auf morgen die Tore schliessen," *Stuttgarter Nachrichten,* 18 June 1973.
"Selbstbezichtigungen," *Der Abend,* Berlin, 27 August 1973.
"Verachtet mir den Bürger nicht," *Die Presse,* Vienna, 12 June 1974.
"Gewissen Illusionen nachzujagen," *Stuttgarter Zeitung,* 14 February 1975.
"Erinnerung ist politische Arbeit," *Die Zeit,* Zurich, 2 January 1976.
"Abkehr von gestern?" *Der Abend,* Berlin, 21 July 1977.
"Utopia as the past conserved" (an interview with Peter Stein and Dieter Sturm by Jack Zipes), *Theater,* New Haven, vol. 9, no. 1 (1977), pp. 50–7.
"Die Verbesserung der Welt durch Melancholie," *Theater heute,* 1979/1, pp. 15–16. (First published *Basler Nachrichten,* 8 July 1978).

INTERVIEWS WITH AND ARTICLES ON STEIN'S ACTORS

Bruno Ganz: "Auffassungen zur Theaterarbeit" (interview by Christoph Kuhn and Peter Meier), *Spielplatz*, ed. Karlheinz Braun and Klaus Völker, Berlin, 1 (1972) 52–71. (First published *Tages-Anzeiger-Magazin*, Zurich, no. 14, 8 April 1972. Reprinted in: Kreuzer, pp. 165–71.)
Therese Giehse: "*Ich hab nichts zum Sagen*" *Gespräche mit Monika Sperr*, Bertelsmann Verlag, Munich, 1977.
Jutta Lampe: *Theater heute*, 1972/13, pp. 107–9; 1978/13, pp. 28–30.
Libgart Schwarz: *Theater heute*, 1978/13, pp. 20–2.

OTHER SOURCES

Unpublished taped interview with Peter Stein by Rudolf Bergmann at the Schaubühne, Summer 1978.
Protocols of discussions and rehearsals at the Schaubühne, 1970 onwards.
Video tapes of *Im Dickicht der Städte* (Norddeutscher Rundfunk), *Torquato Tasso* (Norddeutscher Rundfunk), *Struwelpeter* (Sender Freies Berlin), *Die Mutter* (Sender Freies Berlin), *Peer Gynt* (Allgemeine Rundfunkanstalten Deutschlands), *Optimistische Tragödie* (Westdeutscher Rundfunk), *Prinz von Homburg* (Sender Freies Berlin), *Das Sparschwein* (Sender Freies Berlin), *Antikenprojekt I*.
Films of *Saved* (*Gerettet*, 1967), *Summerfolk* (*Sommergäste*, 1976), *Shakespeare's Memory* (1977), *As You Like It* (*Wie es euch gefällt*, 1978), *Trilogie des Wiedersehens* (1978), *Gross und klein* (1979). (Only *Sommergäste* and *Gross und klein* have been released for general distribution.)

Index